Irv! Buffalo's Anchorman

The Irv, Rick, & Tom Storv

By Steve Cichon

To RITA -

I KNOW YOU WILL "LIKE" THIS BOOK

Steve Cichon

STEVE CICHON

ISBN: 978-0-9828739-0-8

Published by staffannouncer.com, Buffalo, NY

Distributed by Western New York Wares.

Table of Contents

i. Forward   4

1. Irv, Rick, and Tom   6

     The Eyewitness News Game   10

2. Irwin Weinstein, Junior Announcer   11

     Da-di-Da... IRV!   35

3. Ricardo Carballada, Actor   37

4. Tom Jolls, Country Boy   55

     The Eyewitness News Rap   68

5. The Eyewitness News Team is Born   70

6. Topping Tonight's Eyewitness News...   102

     Do You Have This in Blue?   129

7. Beyond the News   130

About the Author   144

Acknowledgements   145

About the Publisher   148

Forward

What an honor it is to write the story of Buffalo's all-time most popular and acclaimed media personalities and news team.

About 6 years ago, I posted an 'Irv, Rick, & Tom' page on my Buffalo *pop culture* history website, staffannouncer.com. It remains one of the most popular pages on the site, and one of the stories I'm most proud to have put on the web.

I grew up in Buffalo and Western New York in the 1980s. Irv, Rick and Tom were a big part of that. While many fathers and sons bond watching sports, from the time I was very small, my dad and I watched the news together every night. Irv's news.

Well before I could actually speak many important words coherently, my mother reports that I, as a toddler, gleefully talked about 'Irv Tine-Tine' and would run around the living room vocalizing the percussive *Eyewitness News* theme at 6pm. Around that time, I also began to realize that Commander Tom, wearing that red jacket with gold epaulets, was quite possibly the coolest guy on the planet wearing the greatest outfit I'd ever seen. And of course, it was a highlight of my young life to meet *THE* Rick Azar at the Broadway Market one Good Friday with my grandma.

One of my early thrills in working in media was as a 15 year old WBEN intern, taking a phone call from Irv each day to record a radio commercial for that night's 6 o'clock news. I also recall several years later, when I was working in a competing Buffalo TV newsroom, the euphoria the day it was announced Irv was retiring; euphoria because *now we have a chance.*

I could really talk about these guys all day, but before I get to embarrassing myself, I've limited my personal comments to one page. There's not a lot of heavy lifting on the pages to follow; hopefully just cause for smiles and memories of the way things used to be, and the story of how Irv, Rick and Tom came to be Buffalo's best ever.

Steve Cichon   sjcichon@aol.com   August, 2011

Rick, Irv, and Tom toast 35 years of Channel 7.
Martin Biniasz photo/Staffannouncer Archives

Chapter 1: Irv, Rick, & Tom.

Chuck Healy. John Corbett. Stephen Rowan. John Beard. Carol Jasen. Bob Koop. Kevin O'Connell. Rich Newberg. Don Postles. That's just a partial list of the folks who appeared as a regular news anchor at 6 o'clock on Channel 4 during Irv Weinstein's tremendous, nearly 30 year run at *Number One* on Channel 7. The list from Channel 2 is three times as long.

So what made Irv so special? It's not an easy question to answer. Irv is loganberry, The Broadway Market, Sahlen's hot dogs, Crystal Beach, Mighty Taco, Jimmy Griffin, knowing how to pronounce Scajaquada, and knowing it connects to not "Route 33," but "*The* 33," all wrapped up into a single 5'7" newsman. Irv is the embodiment of Buffalo.

But really, what makes Irv so special?

A 1990 study of local newscasts scientifically asked several hundred Western New Yorkers a series of in-depth questions about television news in Buffalo.

Without prompting a name, Irv was the runaway favorite news anchor in Buffalo. He was the favorite of more than a third of those with a preference, and was more popular than the numbers 2, 3, and 4 combined. He was the favorite newscaster of young and old, men and women, those making under $25,000, those making $25,000-50,000, and those making above $50,000.

He was the favorite newscaster of those of Polish descent, Italian ancestry, Irish, English, and African-American, too. Also in Buffalo, the Erie County suburbs, Niagara County, and Cattaraugus and Chautauqua Counties, Irv was on top. In every category that was analyzed, Irv Weinstein was a runaway pick as Buffalo's favorite newsman.

One special thing about Irv; you had an opinion of him. He wasn't just a haircut and a baritone reading the news. Of those who had a least favorite news anchor, Irv was named by 44%. He was the favorite, and the least favorite.

But now, over a decade after leaving the Eyewitness News anchor desk, Irv has transcended completely the picayune tastes of Western New York's television watching public.

Just like so many other Buffalo institutions of the past, the name *Irv Weinstein* conjures up different feelings and emotions in different contexts:

Like Bethlehem Steel, Irv reminds people of what a giant Buffalo once was.

Like Crystal Beach, Irv reminds people of the way things used to be; back when life was a little more fun.

Like AM&As or Marine Midland Bank, Irv reminds us that many of our once proud local institutions keep on *keeping on*, but never the way they once were.

O f course, Irv is only a third of the story. It was the combination of Irv, Rick Azar with Eyewitness Sports, and Tom Jolls with the Weather Outside that made Eyewitness News, and each man individually, wildly popular.

"*IrvRickTom* is what we called them," said Phil Beuth, who was Channel 7's General Manager in the 1970's and 80's before moving on to run ABC's *Good Morning America*.

"For many years, that's the way we considered them: *IrvRickTom*, one word, one person. We literally saw them as a seamless team. So close, so well knit so much an extension of one another. "

"It's very hard to define chemistry," Irv said when being inducted into the Buffalo Broadcasting Hall of Fame with Rick and Tom, "but we had it almost immediately, the three of us."

Viewers saw not only news, sports and weather, but also three guys enjoying each others' company, kidding around a little bit between segments.

Each complimented the other perfectly. Paired with others, Irv may have been too brash; Rick might have seemed too slick and polished; Tom maybe a little too folksy. But the honest human interaction between each of these men, as they came into our homes at dinner time and again at bed time, was so obviously real, and so obviously reflective of the people in our own lives, we accepted them as members of our family in a way that no other Buffalo television personalities had been accepted before, and none likely ever will again.

"You had Tom, every mother's son; the flag, and apple pie, and all of those things that make for a fine American," says Irv. "That's what you saw, that's what you got. That's what Tom was, that's what Tom is.

"Rick was more of a broadcasting personality," says Irv in analysis of his anchor desk compadres. "Solid professional, knowledgeable, debonair, good looking guy. Very smooth, Mr. Smooth, the Latin Lover."

So where does Irv fit in?

"Me? I'm an ethnic type," says Irv. "Definitely an ethnic type. I felt very proud of the fact in a heavily Catholic, heavily Polish town, this Jewish kid was accepted."

The mix of these three seemingly disparate characters, added to the humble beginnings of the team on WKBW-TV in the mid-60s, makes the fact that Irv, Rick and Tom are adored two decades after the team broke up even more improbable.

Irv likes to say when he started at WKBW-TV; it was the *number 4* station in a three station market. He often quips, "The ratings at Channel 7 were worse than the sign-off test patterns on Channels 4 and 2." That's not that far from the truth.

Irv moved from WKBW Radio to WKBW-TV in April 1964. Rick Azar was already there. He was the announcer who literally signed the station on the air in 1958. Tom Jolls had been working at WBEN Radio and TV, when Red Koch, the program director at 7, talked Tom into coming over to WKBW's Main Street studios in 1965.

Dear Irv Weinstein:

When did you decide you were going to become a newscaster?

When they told me I would never dance again.

Dear Irv, what exactly is the Weinstein Theory of newscasting?

The Weinstein Theory means accurate reporting, combined with the best on-location news film. It means warm and friendly people like the Eyewitness News team who have been around long enough to really understand what's important to Western New Yorkers. It means communicating better than anybody else.

Dear Irv, what is your favorite TV Program?

The Commander Tom Show, what else?

Dear Irv, where did you work before you came to Buffalo?

My first broadcasting job was in Rochester. I have also worked in California, Oregon and West Virginia. Buffalo has been my home for the past 15 years.

Dear Irv, can you give me your candid opinion of Tom Jolls' wardrobe?

Nice day, isn't it?

KEEP THOSE CARDS AND LETTERS COMING IN, FOLKS

EYEWITNESS NEWS • 6 & 11 PM • WKBW-TV (7)

Buffalo State College Courier Express Collection/Staffannouncer Archives

The Eyewitness Newsgame

Buffalo's own Irv-based board game hit store shelves in 1980, and was available at places like AM&A's and Hengerer's.

Promos showed Irv, Rick, and Tom playing the game so intently, they almost missed the 11 o'clock news.

The box reads:

Your chance to become a junior reporter for Eyewitness News! Be the first back to the station with all the facts and get your story on the air.

Proceeds from the sale of the game went to the Variety Club.

Chapter 2: Irwin Weinstein, Junior Announcer

" As Buffalonians, if we could be smart, we'd want to be smart like Irv," Phil Beuth once said toasting Weinstein. "Smart enough to give us the news, but also using his brilliance to make everyone smile, and to occasionally be a wise guy. He was the smart kid that always made the whole class… except the teacher… laugh. "

A high school teacher told Irv he'd wind up in jail or famous.

So begins a look back at the life of the man that Buffalo lovingly knows as just "Irv."

Despite all the fame and success associated with Eyewitness News, Irv counts another era of his broadcasting career as the "most thrilling and glamorous."

At a time before there was any such person as *Irv Weinstein*, Irwin B. Weinstein was a *big man on campus* at Ben Franklin High School in Rochester, because of his regular appearances on the biggest radio station in town.

"I had actually started at WHAM radio in Rochester as a boy actor. That was perhaps the most thrilling and glamorous part of my entire life in broadcasting. My gosh, I would see these announcers, who go into the booth, once or twice an hour, dressed in a suit, shirt, and tie; and deliver into the microphone the call letters of the station. And that's pretty much all they did. And they were making tremendous salaries. It convinced me, at that time, that this was a profession that I would want to pursue. It wasn't the money; I would have paid for the opportunity to be an announcer."

WHAM was founded by Kodak's founder George Eastman, and was later sold to Stromberg-Carlson, a dominant and wealthy player in the manufacture of radio and telephone equipment.

"WHAM was one of the most prestigious radio stations in the country," remembers Irv. It was (and is) a powerful 50,000 watt station that can be heard all around eastern North America.

Buffalo State College Courier Express Collection/Staffannouncer Archives

"They had, in the mid-40s, a palatial station. One studio could hold an audience of two or three hundred people, had a raised stage, a control room off of the stage, and room for a studio orchestra."

After answering an ad in the newspaper looking for teenagers willing to act on the radio, the man who'd 25 years later be Buffalo's top newsman became a kid playing bit parts in radio dramas; and loving every minute of it.

"In those days, they would call me up, and say, 'We have a part for you as a state trooper,' in a series called *True Stories of the New York State Police*. Because my vocal equipment was pretty much developed at 15 or 16, I would play adults—a state trooper, a bank robber, a farmer in Weedsport who was directing police to the scene of a crime."

"I was getting $7 a show, which was pretty good money for a kid in the mid-1940s. Plus, I was a star at Ben Franklin High School."

Young Irwin was one of *The WHAM Junior Players* as well, on a show that was mostly young people performing basic comedy skits. "It was similar to the things you'd see on sitcoms today", says Irv, "except they'd run 5 or 7 minutes instead of a half hour."

Memories of those days; the raw thrill of scripts flying, last minute changes, and being a teen actor couldn't even be matched as Irv became the most celebrated personality in the history of Buffalo television.

"Possibly the apogee of my career at WHAM was when they brought down some of the network shows to Rochester. They had done some remodeling at the station, and one of the shows they brought to originate from Rochester was *the Henry Aldrich Show*. It was a radio sitcom, and Henry Aldrich was supposed to be a 16 or 17 year old kid. The actor was, in actuality, a man about 40 years old named Ezra Stone."

"My line was four words. I was the Ace Cleaners Boy. You heard the screen door open, and I scream up into the house, 'Ace Cleaners, Mrs. Aldrich!' and she yells back, 'They're in the closet, Harry.'

Irv onstage at "The Playhouse" with actress Tess Spangler, 1980
*Irv and his wife Elaine co-owned the highly-acclaimed
downtown Buffalo theatre with Bryna & Joe Weiss*
Buffalo State College Courier Express Collection/Staffannouncer Archives

"This was pre-audio tape. They did two live shows, one for the east coast, one for the west coast. I was fine for the east coast, but for the west coast, 3 hours later, I blew one of the four words; which has embarrassed me my entire professional life. I don't remember what word it was... maybe 'cleaners.' That would have been a difficult word for me at that stage. But I've never forgotten it. Those are the things that happen in your career that are of such an embarrassing level, that you just never forget it."

"Nobody ever mentioned salary, and that was fine. I just thought they needed me for a bit part in this show, and that was fine. Now, about a month later, an NBC envelope arrives in the mail. The letter says, 'Thank you for taking part in the production of the *Henry Aldrich Show*,' and with it, a check for $230. Again, if there was any doubt about what I wanted to do with my life, $230 for 4 words? It was pointed out to me years later, that Winston Churchill wasn't making that much for his speeches around the same time. I just had a great time."

This was the big time for a high school kid during the mid-1940s; as big, he thought, as it could possibly get. "There was a chief announcer at WHAM at the time, Bill Hanrahan, who was leaving for New York City and NBC."

Hanrahan would go on to be an NBC staff announcer for the next 40 years, best known as the voice of the *Huntley-Brinkley Report*, and later *NBC Nightly News*. His voice became synonymous with not only nightly news broadcasts, but with special news programs involving elections, political conventions, Watergate, and space and lunar exploration.

To young Irwin, however, Hanrahan couldn't have done much better than the biggest station in the *Lilac City*. "I can remember thinking to myself, 'Guy must be crazy! How could he want to leave a great job like this to go to NBC?!?' That was my serious thought."

It was also his serious thought that the glamour of WHAM was the life for him.

"When I got out of school, I thought that the natural thing was, I had worked two or three years at WHAM, and maybe there might be a job for me there. The chief announcer interviewed me, and he advised me that radio probably wasn't the best vehicle for any future career for me. He just didn't think I had it."

At 18, it was the first of many professional let-downs for Weinstein.

Hollywood!

Right after graduating from Rochester's Ben Franklin High School, with no promise of a radio career on the horizon, teenager Weinstein hopped a train to Hollywood, with the idea of breaking into the movies.

"It was a two and a half day trip by train. Rochester to Chicago on the *Empire State Limited*, and then changed to the *Santa Fe Railroad* for the rest of the trip," Irv recalls; a trip that might have gone by faster with a little company. That's the way it was planned, but it didn't work out that way.

"I had a high school buddy who was going to take the trip with me, but he had chickened out at the last minute, so I was alone. I'd never been away from home. I had $400, which I had strenuously saved for this trip."

He wasn't sure how he was going to *break in*, but thought it might be easier than it actually turned out to be. "I didn't think I would just walk in and they would sign me up to a long term contract, but I thought if I got an audition, *maybe*... I just had no idea, I didn't have a clue."

It was true in the 1940s just as it's true today. Just about everyone in Los Angeles is an actor, writer, producer or director; even if they are shampooing your carpets or rolling you a burrito between jobs "in the business."

Buffalo State College Courier Express Collection/Staffannouncer Archives

My Son...the Newscaster

When my son Irv Weinstein was just a curly-headed baby, I knew then he was an unusual child. He learned to talk at an early age, using such big words as "alleged", "eyewitness", "reliable sources" and "Da-Da". I hoped he might someday be a brain surgeon, an accountant, or even own his own delicatessan. Little did I dream that my lovable Irv would someday be the most popular newscaster in Western New York. If you want to make a mother happy, watch a newscaster that's a <u>newscaster</u>! Watch Irv Weinstein . . . he's a good boy.

EYEWITNESS NEWS·6&11PM·WKBW-TV

Buffalo State College Courier Express Collection/Staffannouncer Archives

Irv found this out when the man who kept him from becoming a literal "starving artist" delivered him his greatest brush with Hollywood greatness.

"Now I wasn't drinking that young, but I met a bartender, whose bar was near the place where I had a room. They served food, which was free. If you bought a drink; you got a sandwich. So I'd have a ginger ale, and have lunch."

"I struck up a friendship with this bartender, who had told me that he was once an assistant director at Columbia Pictures. And, as young and unsophisticated as I was, I thought to myself, 'Yeah right, and the moon is made of green cheese.'"

"One day he calls me up and says, 'Irwin, ' -which is what my name was at the time, before I changed it professionally to Irv- 'Irwin, how would you like to go to the studio?'"

"I said, 'Sure,' I put on my bar mitzvah suit, and we went out to Columbia Pictures. The whole time, I'm thinking this guy is pulling my chain. We go to the gate, the guy says, 'Hey Art, how ya doin?'"

"Holy Mackerel, I thought to myself, this guy really did work here. We go into the studio, and go to a sound stage, where they're shooting a *Tarzan* movie, with Lex Barker and Denise Darcel. Cheetah was on Lex Barker's shoulder, and, well, did a doo-doo, so they had to stop the scene."

"I'm just glowing with pride. He introduced me to Lex Barker, and Denise Darcel, and then he said, I think Bob Mitchum is shooting a film at another sound stage."

"So we go to that sound stage, and there's Mitchum, and Janet Leigh, shooting a scene from a movie called *Holiday Affair*. I was stunned. They had recreated a part of Central Park for this scene. "Art says to me, 'When they break this scene, we'll go to Bob's trailer and I'll introduce you.' You can imagine what this is for an 18 year old kid from Rochester, NY. The scene breaks, we go to the trailer, and Mitchum says, 'Hey Art!' and he says, 'Mitch, I'd like to introduce you

Irv Weinstein Collection/ Staffannouncer Archives

to a young friend of mine, Irwin Weinstein, who's out here trying to get into the business.' Now, Mitchum was probably about 6-foot-5, and I pull myself up to my complete 5-foot-7, maybe 5-7-and-a-half in heels. He sticks out his hand, 'Good to meet you, Irwin,' 'Thanks, Bob.' Then he asks, 'How 'bout a drink?'"

"Well, sure, I said, thinking, 'I always have a drink at 9 in the morning to hold myself together.' He pours me a gin, vodka, I don't know what it was. But I was drinking it very slowly, believe me."

"Finally, I'm thinking to myself, this is the opportunity of my life to talk to a professional and get a real answer. My voice raised several octaves when I asked, 'Well, Bob, how do you get into this business?' and he looked down at me and said, 'To tell you the truth, I can't tell ya. I'm having a hell of a time staying in the business. There's always somebody climbing up the grease pole behind you.'"

"I thought to myself, well, he's just kind of mentally patting me on the head. I wasn't angry or anything, it's just what I thought. This is great; at least I'll have some great stories to tell my family."

"Years later, when I really got into broadcasting, and I met some people in the business, and I had a greater variety of life experiences, I realized that he was being absolutely straight with me."

"You are never, no matter how big you are, in the movies, in radio, in television, secure. There's always somebody climbing up that grease pole behind you. You never have total security. From that time on, Mitchum, not just as an actor, has been one of my idols."

In the end, he spent a year and a half in California, with nary a sniff at the silver screen; working instead at a shirt factory, department store warehouse, and meat packing plant.

"The closest I got to being in the movies, was at the Pantages Movie Theatre on Hollywood Boulevard watching Kirk Douglas up on the screen in the movie *Champion*."

Leaving Hollywood, Irv was left with figuring out what to do next.

"At the point that it became obvious that the world was not waiting for a short, *facially challenged* kid for a starring role in an MGM musical, I had to change direction."

A decade before the Queen City sat enraptured as he informed us of spectacular blazes, and careening cars; Irv was a furniture store salesman, worked odd jobs, and kept his hand in the business as a part-time vacation fill-in disc jockey.

"I was into my 20s, when I went to the School of Radio and Television Technique in New York City. I thought to myself, growing up in a middle class Jewish home, that maybe I should be doing something more practical than acting."

Television, Take 1

The impudent child taking in this story might be asking, "Is this where Irv becomes a big TV star?"

The answer, with a grandfatherly chuckle is, no, not yet. After learning the finer points of television production, Weinstein broke into the nascent medium not as an anchorman, but as a director. That is, the man who calls the camera shots and runs a broadcast from a technical standpoint.

It was another difficult and humble beginning.

Irv as Technical Director

"My first TV job was in Waterloo, Iowa. I took a bus out there for the interview. I didn't

Buffalo State College Courier Express Collection/Staffannouncer Archives

even have a job offer, and I took a bus. I sent out about 2,000 resumes, and I got 3 replies. One was at KWWL-TV in Waterloo, another was at a station in Missoula, Montana, and I don't remember the third."

It was an inauspicious beginning to the now-celebrated Irv Weinstein television career.

"I went out to Waterloo, and I got a job as a director. I wasn't a very good director."

After only 90 days of working in television, Irv was once again on the outside looking in.

"Basically, directing in television is hitting the right button and thinking very quickly," Irv explained. "I lacked the digital facility. So, three months later, I was fired."

There was little else to do but look for another job.

Young TV director Irwin Weinstein and his bride, Elaine, on their wedding day. Flanked by Irv's mom (left), and Elaine's grandmother (right).

"I was married by that time, and Elaine and I took a barnstorming tour across the country, from Waterloo, Iowa, to my in-law's home in Miami Beach. I have to say, my wife 'the saint' was very supportive during this difficult time. I hit every station, big market, small market, medium market, nothing. I have a memory of changing my pants on a road outside of St. Louis for an interview with a big station there, nothing."

There were no television jobs to be had, but there was the comfort of home.

"We wound up in Miami Beach, and sponged off my in-laws for three months, and decided that wasn't working. So we moved back to Rochester and sponged off my parents."

During this rough patch, Irv Weinstein, later to be known as a peerless purveyor of staccato alliteration, tried to "go straight."

"I had a couple of jobs. One was as a paint salesman for Sears Roebuck; after about a month, the supervisor said to me, 'Irwin, you don't seem to have the Sears spirit.' I said, 'You know what, you're absolutely right,' and I can't tell you how happy I was to get out of there. "

Fate almost landed Irv a life as a civil servant; until Mrs. Weinstein stepped in.

"I was offered a job as a permanent at the Post Office. I had been working there as a temporary. I came home and told Elaine, 'Hey, I could make a hundred and a quarter a week, steady, very secure.' She said, 'That's very nice, but I didn't marry you because I wanted to be married to a Post Office worker.'"

Reinforced and re-energized in trying to make it in the world of show business, Irv went back to work, making contacts, sending out resumes, and finally landing work.

"I got a job at a UHF station, WTAP in Parkersburg, West Virginia. Elaine at this time was 7 months pregnant. It was a terrible station then, and I was again hired as a director."

"Again, three months later, I was fired; only this time there was a complication: In the interim, Elaine had given birth to our son, Marc. I'm thinking, 'this is awful.' Maybe I'm in the wrong business. Maybe I'll go back to Rochester, and my mother will have some hot soup and some comforting words."

But once again, it was because of the love and support of Elaine Weinstein that the Irv Weinstein story continues.

She encouraged Irv to go knock on the door of a radio station and ask for a job. It was to be the easiest job he'd ever received.

"I wound up at WCEF Radio. C-E-F stood for Clarence E. Franklin, who was the station owner, general manager, sales manager, chief engineer, *and* he had a show on the air called the 'Friendly Frank Show.'"

"I asked him if he had any openings, he said, 'When can you start?' I asked, 'Don't you want to audition me?' to which he replied, 'Nah, I know an announcer when I see one.' So, there I was, at WCEF."

It was there, in the mountains of West Virginia, that Irv took on what he considers the "watershed job of his career." For $60 a week, *for the first time ever,* he was a newscaster, but he wasn't yet *Irv Weinstein.*

Borrowing the name of his infant son Marc Robert, Irwin Weinstein became *Mark Roberts* on the air.

Buffalo State College Courier Express Collection/Staffannouncer Archives

"I was about 27 years old the first time I did news. It was interesting, the station was a daytimer. I did news from 9 in the morning, for about 6 hours."

"But then late in the afternoon, I hosted a music show called, *Candlelight and Gold*. Now this was a rock and roll station, but I really loved doing the news."

After a week or so as the station's only news anchor, he was named news director, even though, says Irv, "I was the only one doing news at the station; I was essentially director over myself."

"I was there about a year, and continued to send out resumes, when I got a call from WBOY-TV in Clarksburg. I got the job there, and I found myself directing again. Not doing very well at it, but directing none the less."

But Irv wasn't to spend too much longer as a TV director, and his family wasn't to spend too much longer in West Virginia.

WKBW Futursonic Radio

So it's 1958, and Irv Weinstein is finally a newsman. But he's not Irv Weinstein yet: On the air, he's known as *Mark Roberts*. But he's also in the coal mining country of Clarksburg, West Virginia, a situation he was looking to change.

"I got a call from a good friend of mine, a deejay, Russ Syracuse. Well, Russ *"The Moose"* Syracuse had gotten a job at KB Radio. He told me there was an opening in the newsroom. I told him I didn't have much experience, but he told me to send in a tape."

"The Program Director, Dick Lawrence, got my tape, we exchanged a few calls, and I was very anxious to get out of West Virginia. There was no way we were going to raise our son in the Mountain State, and Buffalo was an ideal market, close to family in Rochester."

PULSE BEAT BUFFALO.... 1520

Irv Weinstein is a radio newsman with a watch and two watchwords—speed and accuracy. Unique in news work, a man whose entire training and background has been in radio, the news director of WKBW is a modern minute man. Minutes are the pulse beat of his approach—an approach that keeps WKBW first in news in its listener area with two five minute, fast breaking newscasts an hour, 24 hours a day.

Heading up a staff of five men who are on-the-spot reporters with an eye on the clock, Weinstein also has a network of correspondents who can put him within thirty miles of any news break in the United States. WKBW's red and white news cars are as familiar as fire engines on the streets of Buffalo and the highways of Western New York. Chasing spot coverage of everything from police news to political conventions, the cars and their newsmen-broadcasters travel better than a quarter-of-a-million miles a year. The results are a scope of coverage that makes WKBW consistently first with the news in the Buffalo area. The variety of WKBW's coverage—farm, city, state and national—reflects Irv's own experience. He learned radio news in New York City, the farm lands of Iowa, the industrial sections of West Virginia and in the coastal cities of California.

He made Buffalo's news interests a study in depth. What do WKBW's listeners want to hear on their newscasts . . . what are the fastest shortcuts to accurate reporting in Western New York . . . what sources have the behind-the-scenes stories? Weinstein and his staff of news experts found the answers to those questions and the results are news as it is made, on the air in seconds with the professional analysis that puts the listener in the picture.

WKBW RADIO BUFFALO
1520 / 50,000 WATTS / A CAPITAL CITIES STATION

OTHER CAPITAL CITIES STATIONS: WKBW-TV, Buffalo, N.Y.
WPAT, N.Y.C. — (Paterson, N.J.)   WPRO and WPRO-TV, Providence, R.I.
WROW, Albany, N.Y.   WTEN-TV, Albany, N.Y.   WTVD-TV, Raleigh-Durham, N.C.

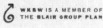

JOHN BLAIR & COMPANY   WKBW IS A MEMBER OF
National Representative   THE BLAIR GROUP PLAN

Irv Weinstein Collection/Staffannouncer Archives

Thus began Irv's news career in Buffalo. But once again, it almost didn't happen.

As Irv told Sandy Beach on *Majic 102* in 1988, "I drove into the parking lot of KB Radio in a beat up *DeSoto*. Dick Lawrence called me in Clarksburg, West Virginia, and he told me I got the job."

"So we loaded up the *DeSoto*, all of our furniture, Elaine and Marc (their son), and we drove up to Buffalo. We get to Buffalo, and I pull into the parking lot, go in and tell the receptionist that I'm here to see Mr. Lawrence. She says, 'well, Mr. Lawrence is no longer with us.'

It was another of those moments you just can't make up.

"My whole life began to pass in front of my eyes. Elaine is out in the parking lot with our infant son, all of our possessions are in the car, and I'm thinking to myself I'm out of a job. I quit this great job, making $75 a week in Clarksburg, and here I am; out of a job, again."

"I seriously may have been hyperventilating when Clint Churchill, Junior, the son of the owner, walked out into the hall, wanting to know 'what's happening here.' I explained the situation, and he said to me, 'Don't worry, you've got a job.'"

"Whew, I thought, catching my breath. 'Can you do the next newscast?,' he asked. 'Certainly,' I said, though maybe I wasn't quite so certain. I was wearing jeans, I really wasn't prepared."

"But 10, 15 minutes later, I did the next newscast, and the rest of the newscasts; apparently someone had just left. At that time, KB Radio had newscasters and news writers, people who wrote the newscasts. That day, the person who was writing the casts was Art Wander. That's enough to make a guy nervous right there, *the Tiny Tot of the Kilowatt.*"

"He wrote one of these wild stories about an accident, where the victim was killed. He wrote that she was whiplashed to death. Well, at that point, I didn't even know my name. Whiplashed to death?!? Well, I read it, what was I going to do? I didn't even have a chance to pre-read the copy."

"So I get off the air, and Churchill called me into his office. He said to me, 'I heard your newscast.' He said it was ok. He said, 'This is a top 40 station, and you sound too much like Walter Cronkite.' I'm thinking, 'and that's a bad thing?'"

"My whole terrible broadcast career passed before my eyes, but luckily it worked out."

That early boss may have tossed the name *Walter Cronkite* his way, but it was another famous radio host who made an impression on Irv.

"In terms of style, I was sometimes asked who my idol was in radio, and that was an easy one: Paul Harvey. Paul Harvey was not fast paced, but he had a pace of delivering the news that was compelling. I like to think I was Paul Harvey only a lot faster."

Faster… with flagrant, more outrageous writing. It might be hard to believe for those who don't remember, but in the early rock 'n' roll days of KB Radio and *Pulsebeat News*, the pace and the *shocking* pointed style of news writing and delivery made Irv's later *Eyewitness News* persona seem comatose.

It took some time to develop that sound, though. Irv readily admits, when he first arrived at KB, he sounded different. "My style was upbeat, but not the on-air style that I developed; which was basically, a Top 40 news guy; fast paced."

Irv Weinstein Collection/ Staffannouncer Archives

It was in its fetal stage, but it was early development of the personality Buffalo would come to cherish over the next 50 years. It was also at KB Radio that Irwin first unwrapped a sleeker sounding version of his first name, and became forever more *Irv*.

"Over time I developed a writing style that had sizzle and alliteration, and the type of thing to grab the audience. I learned along the way, that before you can get people to listen to you, you have to catch their attention. One way to do that is in your writing-- make it compelling. Sometimes it was overboard, frankly, but it was ok. It did the job."

It was the perfect comingling of man and circumstance that put Irv in the position to really invent the style of newscasting he made famous in Buffalo; one that was copied around the country.

Irv wins a Lancaster Speedway Demolition Derby. Danny Neaverth (in a hat), and Fred Klestine (middle) cheer him on.

Danny Neaverth Collection/Staffannouncer Archives

"My theatre background had a lot to do with it. I understood what they wanted. They wanted the listeners to barely discern the difference between Russ *The Moose* Syracuse and Irv Weinstein in terms of basic sound; the pace. And that was fine with me."

News was still serious; different from the disc jockeys. But the KB newsmen, and Irv in particular, would leave that line blurred.

"Russ Syracuse would try to break me up during the news; he'd walk by the studio window doing an imitation of a fish. I must have had a death wish, because we had a cough switch, but I never hit it; I'd just laugh on the air. We used to get requests at the station, people wondering when I was going to laugh."

Were it just his delivery, reading scripts written for him by Art Wander and others, Irv would still be remembered today. But it's that unparalleled ability to turn a phrase while churning out news copy that was to become synonymous with Irv Weinstein over the next four decades of informing Buffalo.

"Again, I discerned what they wanted; and I gave them that, plus. I've often been quoted with lines like 'Pistol packing punks pounded a Polish plumber into the pavement.' I never, ever said anything like that. Close, but that phrase, 'pistol packing punks....' We did some outrageous things on radio."

"I think the news was an integral part of KB Radio's enormous success. There were a lot of rock stations around, but I think what really defines a station, what gives it some personality, some credibility, is the news. People hear the news, they trust the newscaster. KB knocked off WBEN Radio, and it took a while, with people like Clint Buehlman so entrenched, but we knocked off the other stations."

KB was 'number one' across the board, one of the most successful radio stations in the country. Without question; Syracuse, Dan Neaverth, Tom Shannon, Joey Reynolds, Stan Roberts, and all the KB disc jockeys are due much of the credit for that success.

But it would be shortsighted to not also heap credit on Irv, Henry Brach, Jim Fagan, John Zach and all of the *Pulsebeat* Newsmen who gave the gravitas needed to bump off some long established Buffalo legends like Buehlman and newscaster Jack Ogilvie at WBEN among numerous others.

Irv Weinsten Collection/Staffannouncer Archives

Remember, at this point, Irv Weinstein was a *radio* newsman. He could go shopping at the A&P or grab a coffee at a Deco lunch counter without fans mobbing him. His *voice* was familiar; his *face*, not so much.

Early on, after having listened to Irv and his big voice, people were surprised whenever he made public appearances. People heard that booming authoritative voice come through the radio; meeting the diminutive Irv in person didn't always quite seem analogous.

"A Rabbi sent me a note after meeting me for the first time," Irv recalls. "He wrote, 'You know, you're a very talented young man, because after listening to you for so many years, I've always pictured you as a tall, blonde Gentile.' I wrote him back a similarly funny note."

Soon, all of Buffalo would know exactly what Irv looked like.

Da-di-Da… IRV!

Part of the experience of going to a Bisons game at North AmeriCare Park in the late 1990s was the 7th inning stretch presentation of Gary Glitter's *Rock and Roll (Part 2)*, where it was understood instead of yelling "Hey!" for the refrain, the ballpark yelled "Irv!" in unison, as a pixilated image of Buffalo's favorite newsman flashed on the scoreboard. It was all part of one of the last great promotional campaigns for Irv and Eyewitness News.

STEVE CICHON

Buffalo State College Courier Express Collection/Staffannouncer Archives

Chapter 3: Ricardo Carballada, Actor.

Efraim Ricardo Carballada was born on Michigan Avenue on Buffalo's East Side, and was baptized at St. Lucy's on Division Street. But it was the 1930s, and a move to Brooklyn was the first of many for the baby who'd grow up to be one of Buffalo's longest tenured and most beloved broadcasters.

"This was the Depression," says Rick Azar, whose earliest memories are of Brooklyn's streets, though he was born a few blocks from downtown Buffalo. "My father was just moving all around, looking for work."

Among the skills young Rick took away from the hard scrabble streets of the Home of 'Dem Bum' Dodgers-- the ability to play violin, after a guy offered him lessons while he played on a vacant lot with friends.

It was just before World War II that another move would bring the Carballada family back from The Big Apple back to the Queen City.

"My uncle called up my dad and told him they were doing a lot of hiring at Bethlehem Steel," says Azar. As a jack-of-all-trades, he found plenty of work at the bustling plant that put the bread on the tables of thousands and thousands of Buffalo families.

Rick's mom and aunt sold the Brooklyn beauty shop, where that man convinced Rick's mom that the young boy was in need of violin lessons, and it was back to the area around downtown Buffalo, and some familiar landmarks, for the family.

While St. Louis Church still stands as the *mother church* of the Buffalo Catholic Diocese, it was in the long-torn down school, now a vacant lot, where the young pupil Rick came to realize that in front of the bright lights was the place for him.

"Jimmy Cahill, a priest who wasn't much older that we were, ran a very active CYO. We played basketball and softball, but there was a drama group that went back over the years there, The St. Louis Dramatic Society."

"On the third floor of the school," remembers Rick, "they had an auditorium and a stage."

It was on that stage where Father Cahill's friend, a floor manager at the nearby Erlanger Theatre, helped Rick and his friends from St. Louis Grammar School (and later when Rick attended St. Joe's as well) write, rehearse, and act out the plays they'd present in Catholic Youth one-act play contests.

"He started helping us with our plays," Rick remembers with the classic Azar smile in his voice, "and we started winning everything in sight. In the years he was involved, we never placed below first. That's where the acting bug started."

And it was through drama and acting, that Rick picked up his first job in broadcasting.

"I tried out for a dramatic part in a radio play, and I won it."

The first time Buffalo heard the velvety voice of Rick Azar on the air, it wasn't calling touchdowns or free throws, it was a thespian affair on WEBR Radio. From that first part, there were plenty of bits of dramatic work on the radio over the next few years.

Just as young Irwin Weinstein was doing a short train ride away in Rochester, Rick Carballada was earning a few bucks and having fun acting on the radio through his time at St. Joseph's Collegiate Institute and into his time at Canisius College. But it wasn't enough.

"I was wondering what I was going to do with the rest of my life. Father Cahill suggested, 'Why don't you think about radio?'"

So without any better ideas for work, Rick started looking for a summer replacement job not as an actor, but as an announcer, like the ones Irv lusted after at WHAM. But unlike Irv, Rick found some temporary work behind the microphone.

"I had a friend who was a staff announcer at WHLD in Niagara Falls, and I won a summer replacement job out there."

Buffalo State College Courier Express Collection/Staffannouncer Archives

And although it was back to school in September, the next summer there was another radio job, this one closer to home. Rick found himself doing mornings at WWOL in Lackawanna, not too far from his father, who was still working as a millwright at the steel plant.

It was also the summer that Rick bought his first car. *Or at least a share of one.*

"I was in college, and two other guys and I bought a car. We shared it. Two of us put up the money, and we brought the other guy in because he was the only one who knew how to drive. We gave him a piece of the action."

"The three of us would take turns having this car. One day, I had the car. My dad was going to work at the steel plant; I had to go sign-on WWOL at 6am. I said, 'Pa, I'll take you to work, I'll drop you off.'"

"What I didn't know was the night before; the guys had driven to Jamestown and back. We get to the middle of the bridge on Ridge Road, and the car runs out of gas."

What does a good son do? There's only one course of action if that son is a disc jockey with the threat of dead air looming...

"I grabbed my lunch bag, and started running to the station. *I gotta go!* It's about ten minutes to 6, and I have to run because I have to sign the station on the air. I can hear my dad's voice in the distance, 'Wait a minute!'"

It was the only time in 25 years that Rick's dad was late to punch in at Bethlehem Steel, as, alone, he pushed that car to a gas station and waited for the place to open up. By that point, Rick was at a different sort of station.

"I got to the station just as the National Anthem was on, and I was trying to read that first newscast all out of breath."

The job lasted about as long as the car did... Only those fleeting summer months.

Buffalo State College Courier Express Collection/Staffannouncer Archives

A year later, Rick took what he might have expected to be his last ever job in broadcasting, one more time as a summer replacement disc jockey and announcer; this time at Lockport's WUSJ.

It was there, under the name "Rick Corey," that he read some news, some sports, did a disc jockey show, and also enchanted a young Niagara County high school kid who'd hang around the station.

Neither the suave college kid announcer, nor the country boy who would stare at him through the glass, could have fathomed where next they might meet.

"Tom Jolls used to hang around the station," says Rick with an almost big-brother-like perturbedness, recalling 60 years hence the man who'd become his weather-forecasting wingman, ogling him through the studio windows.

There was a hope at WUSJ that Rick might stay on the staff, even after the summer replacement gig was through. Rick, however, had other plans, including his last year at Canisius.

"After I graduated, I had no intention of going into radio," Rick recalls. Instead, with a degree in hand, Rick bolted from Buffalo for Hartford, Connecticut, and a job in the Latin American department of a big fire insurance company.

But actuary tables and open perils clauses didn't have the same sort of pizzazz as play scripts and live audiences. Rick joined a semi-professional theatre group in Hartford, when his acting caught the eye of a New York City director.

"I was in a play called 'The Silver Cord,' and some director from New York happened to see me. He contacted me, and told me 'You should be in New York.' Boom. Just like that."

With a little bit of money stashed away, Rick retired from the insurance business.

"I had saved a hundred, maybe a hundred-fifty bucks-- Quite a bit of money in those days-- so I said, 'I'm going to New York!'"

"My cousin had a 99 year lease on a rooming house on State Street in Brooklyn, and that's where I lived. Didn't cost me anything, and I tried my luck at being a Broadway actor."

Some bit parts here and there led Rick to Barnesville, Pennsylvania, which in turn lead him to Chicago, just going along with the tide.

The Chicago play went on tour, and Rick saw plenty of the country that summer and fall. "We even played the Erlanger Theatre in Buffalo," says Rick, "which was a real fun thing for me."

What began as some afterschool fun with an Erlanger Theatre connection became a big time job with an Erlanger Theatre connection. Rick was moving up in the New York stage world.

"By this time, I had a legitimate agent who was very interested in my work. Their big name at the time was Imogene Coca, who was a star from the Sid Caeser 'Your Show of Shows.'"

It was that New York City Talent Agent who told Ricardo Carballada that his polysyllabic, *uber-ethnic* name wasn't going to cut it in showbiz.

"You gotta get another name," the New York big shot said. "Nobody'll be able to pronounce that."

As someone who spent time on the radio in his home town under an assumed, easier to pronounce name, the thought wasn't completely unbearable to Rick. But it was important for him that the "made up" name have some semblance of authenticity.

"In those days, everyone changed their name. I was thinking, 'What am I going to call myself?'"

"Most people called me Rick, and that was fine, but I didn't want to be Rick O'Grady or Rick Smith, or some dumb thing that people would know isn't my real name."

Buffalo State College Courier Express Collection/Staffannouncer Archives

"My father came from the northwest corner of Spain, Galicia. I started looking at Spanish names on the map, and I wanted something simple. -AZAR is the last four letters of at least half a dozen Spanish names.... Solazar, Salazar, Alcazar, all -*azar*."

"So I said, Rick Azar. That sounds pretty good to me. And the agent said, 'That's great.' And that's where the name came from.'"

Stan Roberts, Rick, Carroll Hardy, Frank Benny, and Van Miller 'horsing around.' Stan Roberts Collection/Staffannouncer Archives

The touring play which hopped from Chicago to Buffalo's Erlanger Theatre and then points all over the map, finally wrapped in early December. Rick figured he'd go home to Buffalo for an extended Christmas/New Year's break, as a young man connected with a well-known talent agency and a burgeoning stage career ahead of him.

Among the many chums he ran into while pallin' around the Niagara Frontier that December was his old friend Eddy Jo, who, after being on

the air himself for a while, had come to be running WHLD Radio in
Niagara Falls.

"He asked what I was doing, and he said, 'Come to work! We need a
guy right now!'"

"I told him I was going back to New York, but he said, just for a few
months."

Not exactly what the newly-christened Rick Azar had in mind, but it
did make some sense, because he did have a few months, and could
use a little walking around money.

"So thinking about it, April is when they start casting for a lot of
Broadway stuff. I figured I'd take the job for a few months, save some
money, and then head back to New York in April for those Broadway
auditions."

Despite the feeling it was nothing more than a temporary gig, being
back on the radio fit like an old shoe.

"At WHLD I was doing everything. Disc jockey; I started doing some
sports. I went to some big shindig at a big, really well-known nightclub
in Niagara Falls called Luigi's on Ontario Street."

"I ran into a guy I went to high school with, and he was working in
radio over at WJJL. We got to talking, and he asked me if I had any
good contacts in New York, because he had this singer, and he said this
gal is terrific."

"He said, 'See that gal over there in the yellow dress? She's going to
sing later.' I looked at her, and as God as my witness, I said to myself,
'that's the girl I'm going to marry.' And that's the girl I married."

Rick gave up the love of the stage for the love of the girl in the yellow
dress, and never made it back to Broadway. He stayed in the radio job
in Niagara Falls, until opportunity knocked with what turned out to be
his first television job in Buffalo.

WHLD personalities Ramblin' Lou Schriver (left), Lucky Pierre (with microphone), and Rick Azar (with cap). Staffannouncer Archives

"At that time, WBUF-TV, Channel 17, was purchased by NBC, and they were looking for people. I went down there on a lark, and I got the job."

WBUF-TV was Buffalo's second television station, but it struggled as a UHF (channels 14-83) station at a time when TVs being sold only came equipped to receive channels 2-13 without special equipment. When the National Broadcasting Company came into Buffalo to buy WBUF-TV in 1955, it was a short lived boon for the high-numbered station. Though later known as *the Dean of Buffalo TV sportscasters*, the roles of announcers weren't as clearly defined in the earliest days of the then-nascent medium of television.

Buffalo State College Courier Express Collection/Staffannouncer Archives

"I did everything there. I got involved in the sports end of things there, I did the weather, the news, everything."

It was also at WBUF-TV that Rick would meet and work with another young announcer he'd meet again at Channel 7.

"I worked with Dave Thomas there, it was great. We really had a wonderful time."

It was *early* in his television career though, when Rick thought he saw *the end* of his television career flash before his eyes… Or maybe, more appropriately, fall off the tip of his tongue.

"One time, as the sign-off announcer at WBUF-TV, I was watching *"Tonight with Steve Allen,"* and I had a promotional thing I had to read after Steve Allen went off the air around one o'clock."

"It was a real production; remember this is the mid 1950s. They had a film, and I was supposed to read live over a film. The music was on there already, a big fanfare, and then I was supposed to read, 'The events of tomorrow will determine whether we're at *peace* or at war,' except 'peace' came out 'piss.'"

"I thought *oh boy, this is my last job.* The only other guy in the studio was the engineer, and I saw his head slowly look up from the console, looking at me, but I couldn't look at him. I tried to read the thing as quick as I could, to get the hell out of there."

"We laughed and laughed about that, but as far as I can tell, no one heard it. I never heard anything from anyone about what I said on the air that night."

But it really didn't matter anyway, in the long run, because soon thereafter, NBC sold off the station, they went out of business, and Rick was out of a job.

"I've got two babies at home at this time," remembers Rick worrying about being without a gig. A friend got him an interview at a station in Denver owned by Bob Hope, but Denver wasn't the city it is now.

Buffalo State College Courier Express Collection/Staffannouncer Archives

"It was still a cow town then. They treated me well, the audition went well, it was great. They offered me a job, but I said that I'd have to talk it over with my wife. I was standing on the boardwalk at the airport, and there's nothing after that. I look to the east, and the only thing I see is the horizon. I look to the west, and the only thing I can see is the Rocky Mountains."

"The Rocky Mountains are awesome, but they aren't what I'd call 'beautiful.' They're a bit overwhelming. I said to myself, 'Where the hell am I.' I knew I was meant to be an Easterner, and I never took the job."

But it wasn't long before work found him again, this time once again in *the city that never sleeps.*

"I came back to Buffalo, and that same guy called me and said 'Get to New York.'"

NBC in New York had an announcer opening when one of the staff took a leave of absence to host a quiz show. Rick was hired, and became one of 22 staff announcers at NBC in New York City.

"At that time, at Rockefeller Center, you really worked for 4 stations. Local radio, network radio, local TV, and network TV. We were all over the place. We even did tear-off-the-wire news on the radio. There was no news department."

It was the big time, to be certain, but it wasn't home. It made a call coming from the people starting a new television station back home in Buffalo intriguing.

Radio station WKBW owner Dr. Clinton Churchill won a heated battle with the *Courier-Express* for the license for Buffalo's last UHF station, Channel 7. The new TV station would carry the same WKBW call letters that the Methodist Episcopal Minister Churchill proclaimed stood for "Well Known Bible Witness."

The WKBW job offer was a crossroads for Rick. He'd been at NBC New York for 3 months, but was working on a series of 12 week contracts. He needed something more permanent.

"I went to the powers-that-be at NBC, and I said if you can guarantee me work through April, and give me a six month summer replacement job, I'll move to New York, bring my family everything."

"They said, 'Well, I don't know if we can do that,' and I said, 'Well, then you've got two weeks' notice.'"

"They looked at me stunned, but I had my wife and those two babies in Buffalo, and I would fly back on Saturdays whenever I could. I wasn't back in Buffalo two weeks before NBC called me to say, 'Come back.'"

"I said, 'no.'"

"I often think about that, what the hell would have happened; had I stayed in New York on NBC."

"There were a couple of things percolating there. I had become friends with Steve Lawrence, and there was talk of him getting a show, and that I would be the announcer. But I couldn't go on the *if come*."

"I was married, I had two babies, and I loved Buffalo. And I stayed at Channel 7, signed the station on the air November 30, 1958."

Literally signed the station on. The first voice heard on Channel 7 was one viewers would hear daily for the next 31 years.

Buffalo State College Courier Express Collection/Staffannouncer Archives

Buffalo State College Courier Express Collection/Staffannouncer Archives

Chapter 4: Tom Jolls, Country Boy

fire bug touches off both a spectacular blaze and a broadcasting career with a single match....

Tom Jolls read the Eyewitness News Reel for decades, and that's likely the way the story may have started as a *newsreel* item. But instead of announcing the news of the *Niagara County smoker*, eventually, Tom lived it.

An only child, Tom was born in Newfane, and grew up in the Town of Lockport. His dad loaded barrels on railcars, later; he was a foreman at a soap plant.

"Looking back, although I didn't realize it that the time, we were pretty poor growing up," remembers Tom. "It was the 1930s, and my dad was making $18 a week, so we didn't have much. But as I say, I never realized it until I looked back."

His childhood was a wonderful but simple one. The kind Norman Rockwell painted. The kind Tom helped bring through the TV to Western New York children by the thousands.

"I was a country boy, raised in the country; attended a two room country school. I was quite sheltered, really. I didn't have much of a broad background. I was very innocent as to what was going on in the world."

His world was what he found in rural Niagara County at the tail end of the Great Depression.

"Friends on my street and at school, and at the old fishing hole at the end of the street, things like that. Once in a while, we'd go to Olcott Beach, and that'd be the highlight of summer. Maybe once we went to Crystal Beach. Very seldom we came into the big city; maybe at Christmas time we'd come in to downtown Buffalo and do some shopping."

Then the world became a little too real pretty fast, as it did for lots of kids as America went from Depression to fighting Nazism and Imperial Japan.

"The war was going on of course, and then my uncle went into the Army, so I was becoming aware of what was going on worldwide; and constantly lived in fear that something was going to happen to this country."

His early education began in a two-room school house, and his early interest in weather began on the 8 miles round trip he walked each day coming from and going to school in rural Niagara County.

The extreme differences in winter weather left him especially fascinated to the point where he started to keep a running tally. He liked the nice crisp sunny days, chilly, but with no wind and only the sharp crunch of snow under feet to keep him company on that 4 mile trek. It was the other kind of days, though, that seemed to be more plentiful. The days when the wind drove cold and snow through all layers of clothes, leaving school-boy Tom frozen to the core.

Like most Western New York children of the '40s, (and '50s, '60s, and '70s, for that matter), before heading out on the coldest and snowiest of those mornings, he'd tune into WBEN and Clint Buehlman with the hope of hearing that school might be closed.

More often than not, though, for Tom it was just listening to Buehly singing a little song about the weather on his way out the door to head to school and make those weather observations for himself.

Ironically, it would be the end of the long, sometimes painfully cold walks which piqued his interest in weather, which would allow the very earliest seeds of a broadcasting career to sprout.

"An arson fire at our school house burned it to the ground," says Tom, who then began taking lessons at the much more urban North Park Junior High in the City of Lockport. "Had that not happened, my career would have been different."

Tom Jolls Collection/Staffannouncer Archives

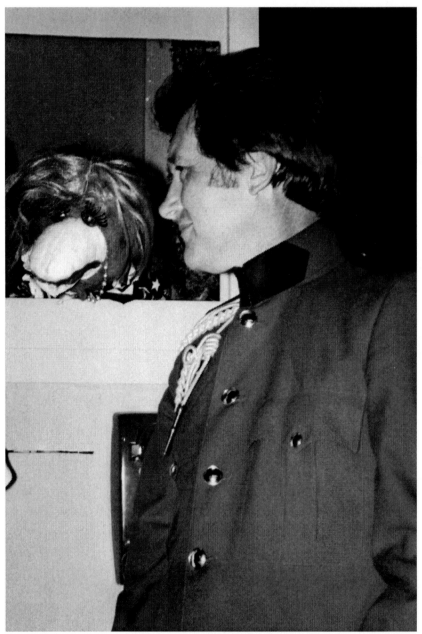

Tom Jolls Collection/Staffannouncer Archives

He went from the school that was an old-fashioned holdover from another time, to climbing behind the microphone every day.

"A dramatics teacher, Miss Canfield, she discovered that I had some sort of a (the Commander uses the finger quotes here) 'talent' for something or another, so she put me on the announcements every morning."

"So at 8 o'clock, I stood on this little stool, right up to the microphone to say 'Good morning,' and then I'd go through the announcements of the day."

This cursory foray into "broadcasting" had really been a long time in coming.

"I had a cardboard cutout microphone, with a string on it, attached to the radio, and I would read the newspaper every night. I was the only child, so I had no siblings to make fun of me, or to ask what I was doing."

Tom got to love the thought of being behind a microphone, and it became a bit of an obsession; especially when, in a field just across the street from his school, the Lockport Union Sun & Journal began building Lockport's first radio station, WUSJ.

"I used to look out the window as say to myself, 'Boy, I'd like to work there someday.'"

He wasn't a staff announcer, but it was a very young Tom who first walked through the doors of WUSJ to deliver over the radio a show he'd worked all week to put together.

"Each Thursday, we'd do a live broadcast called 'Meet the Schools.' I did that right through my senior year of high school."

And it was while doing that show, and hanging around the station, that Tom would meet a guy he'd get to know much better a few years later.

"I was 14 or 15, and Rick Corey was one of the first announcers at the Lockport station in 1948 or '49."

Rick Corey was still 7 or 8 years away from taking the name *Azar* off that map of Spain. Rick remembers Tom as the young hanger-on, but Tom remembers Rick as the cool older guy with a dream job.

"When I was in there doing the school news, I'd stand and watch him through the glass, thinking, 'Oh boy, how lucky he is... I wish I could do something like that some day.'"

And the wish came true soon enough.

"I got to know people at the radio station, they got to know me, and I just started to blend in, and when I graduated from high school, there was an opening. I started as a music librarian on the weekend, but eventually got on the air."

By the time he was fresh out of high school, Tom was on the air from 7am to 3pm every day.

"At WUSJ, I did everything. Even swept the floor, and shoveled the sidewalk, as I jokingly say. Really though, I did news, I did sports, I was a disc jockey, farm reporter, I did the whole thing. It was fun though; it was a great learning experience."

It was right around this time, that Tom made another move that's stuck with him even longer than that desire to get in front of a microphone.

Not too long after graduating from high school, he saw a girl he'd known for a long time, but hadn't exactly won over with his debonair charm. In fact, Tom says, all through school he'd made fun of her and her friends.

"Janice lived not too far from me, we rode the same school bus, and our families shared a 12 person party line on the phone," remembers Tom.

Tom at the GM's desk at WUSJ.
Tom Jolls Collection/Staffannouncer Archives

Nowadays, kids have their own cell phones and call anyone, anytime. But when 12 families share the same phone line, making a phone call often took some planning. Tom took advantage of that.

"Occasionally, I'd hear her say that she was going to talk to a friend at such-and-such a time, so I'd pick up the phone and listen in. Then the next day, I'd repeat some of those things back to her, and she'd get just furious with me."

"After I graduated from high school, I was with some friends, and I saw Janice. I gathered up the courage to ask her out with me, and she said yes."

Like Mrs. Weinstein and Mrs. Azar, Mrs. Jolls has been her husband's trusted co-anchor long before there was even thought of Channel 7, let alone Eyewitness News of Irv, Rick, and Tom.

Tom was also a television pioneer, a decade and a half before he ever said, "Back to you, Irv" on Channel 7.

"Just before I was drafted, I went up to WBES-TV, Channel 59, which was up in the Lafayette Hotel."

It was a fun time for Tom, who got to work with other past and future Buffalo TV and Radio stars like Doris Jones and Roger Baker at the station.

"Roger Baker was a name that went way back in Buffalo radio, especially in sports, and here I am, at 18, doing news for him on WBES-TV! I was really like, 'Wow,' you know?"

But it wasn't meant to last.

"It went bankrupt very quickly. In fact, when I came home from the Army for Christmas leave, I read in the Courier, 'the now defunct WBES-TV,' and I thought, 'What happened! My job is gone!'"

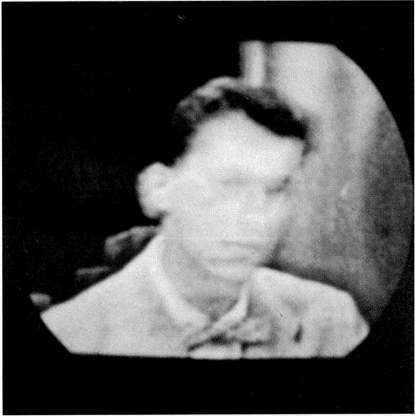

Tom Jolls on WBES-TV, 1956
Tom Jolls Collection/Staffannouncer Archives

But after that hitch with Uncle Sam in the Signal Corps, Tom found a job waiting for him back in Lockport at WUSJ. He put in another decade or so in Niagara County radio, until one of the station's big sponsors told the chief announcer at WBEN how good Tom was.

"Carl Erickson was one of the good friends of one of the owners of Lockport Motors, and he mentioned to Carl that he should come to Lockport and listen to me; he did. He hired me on the spot after doing what I thought was a terrible newscast."

Tom's first job at WBEN Radio and TV was hosting a show that was the creation of WBEN's program director, the same guy who also played Santa Claus on Channel 4.

Buffalo State College Courier Express Collection/Staffannouncer Archives

"My first job at WBEN, I did a radio show from 3 to 4 everyday called Kaleidoscope. This was Bill Peters pride and joy. He developed this, and he wanted to do something different than what was the run of the mill. I would take a theme each day, and run with it, whether it was classical music, if it was Broadway Shows, themes from movies."

Peters loved it, but another vaunted name from WBEN's past wasn't so enthusiastic. Of course, like most stories, Tom Jolls tells this one laughing.

"John Corbett would follow me with *Car and Kitchen*, and sometimes he'd be so mad at a theme that I had, he'd say, 'You're turning off the listeners! Nobody's going to be listening to me!'"

Corbett's show was filled with sponsors, and that's where the money was made at WBEN back in those days.

"We were all staff announcers, really, then if you were lucky enough to get a talent fee for something, well, that was sought after."

Tom's biggest talent fees came from the television end of things, which hadn't quite yet caught up to radio as the more dominant medium.

"I was lucky enough to win the audition for the *Esso Reporter*, so I did the *Esso News* at 11 o'clock on Channel 4. In those days, the news guy did the weather, too."

Talent fee, but this wasn't a cushy anchor job.

"The sponsor, Esso, wanted me to work every day. I had to work 7 days a week. Monday and Tuesday were my days off, but I had to go in to do the news at 11 on those nights, so I really had no time off."

It really made the next step in his career easy enough for him, though there may have been a little hand wringing.

"When Channel 7 offered me a job doing weather, and weekends off, I thought, 'Wow!'"

But remember, that at in 1964, Channel 7 was the distant third station in the market, with the distant third network ABC. Channel 4 was the dominant heritage number one station, with the number one network, CBS.

"I'll never forget the reaction from the chief engineer at WBEN when he found out I was leaving. 'Do you know what you're doing?' he asked. 'You're leaving *this* for *that*?'"

"Of course in the long run, it turned out to be the best thing I ever did. But it was a very long, drawn out process of trying to decide what I was going to do."

"Was I going to stay at 4, WBEN, the rock of the broadcast business, or am I going to go off to this third rated station, and as it turned out..."

Tom Jolls Collection/Staffannouncer Archives

STEVE CICHON

Eyewitness News Rap

© 1987 Words By Mike Randall, Music By Dick Bauerle

They've been the best in the business for a very long time
I've been watching them myself since I was only nine
They're the longest running anchor team in history
And they're the only news team I want on my TV.

My name is Tom Jolls, but you can call me CT
When you want to know the weather you can count on me
I do it outside, because that's where it's at
My rap is finished, so Rick's up to bat!

My name is Azar, that's Rick for short
I've got the inside scoop on every sport
I tell it like it is, the way you deserve
So does this man, our main man Irv!

Listen party people and don't be late
You'll always get the scoop; I give it to you straight
I'll give you the news that you need to know,
On Western New York's number one news show!

You see me with Irv, I'm Mary McCombs
I like bringing the news into your homes
You know your health is a concern of mine.
My healthwatch reports will make you feel just fine!

That's the Eyewitness News team and this is their story
It's a news tradition; it's a tale of glory
Watch them every night; they'll let ya know what's happening
Eyewitness News is the best! That's the point of all this rappin!

Buffalo State College Courier Express Collection/Staffannouncer Archives

Chapter 5: The Eyewitness News Team is Born

WKBW-TV officially signed on the air at 2:30 on a Sunday afternoon. November 30, 1958 was a lazy, snowy Buffalo day, the kind of day where maybe you'd turn on the TV set to see the new channel sign on for the first time.

There wasn't much fanfare, though, as the switch was flipped. The Buffalo Courier-Express, perhaps still sore that it didn't receive the license for Buffalo's final VHF station, didn't even cover the fact that WKBW-TV was signing on the day that it happened.

The Buffalo Evening News carried a few brief articles in the Saturday paper, but the only story in that week's TV Topics was a small one, on the fourth page, talking about the announcers that Buffalonians might recognize on the station about to sign on.

Among those mentioned, was "RICK AZAR, WEATHERMAN." A brief biographical sketch outlined his work at local radio stations, and the defunct WBUF-TV.

It was the voice of Rick, Channel 7's first weatherman, which broke through the test pattern with the words, "Ladies and Gentlemen, WKBW-TV Channel 7 is on-the-air!"

After a brief "dignified statement of hopes, purpose, and sense of responsibility" by station owner Dr. Clinton Churchill, the first entertainment on the station was the 1942 film "Yankee Doodle Dandy."

The next day, the only press coverage of the sign-on was in two short paragraphs in the Buffalo Evening News, saying the station signed on with a "smooth professional competence."

And although owner and Methodist Minister Dr. Churchill said upon sign on, "we will endeavor at all times to bring you the finest in television entertainment and public service," the station was certainly firmed planted as the last resort for Buffalo television viewers in those early years.

Among Rick's original duties at Channel 7: Hosting local teen dance show "Buffalo Bandstand."

Buffalo State College Courier Express Collection/Staffannouncer Archives

The national offerings from ABC were third rate at best, with many shows, notably westerns, appealing more to kids than their parents.

And the local staff was small. Five announcers, who did all the station breaks and announcements live, all day long, but also doubled as news and weather people on the nightly newscasts.

"We did everything," remembers Rick Azar. "I was doing the weather, and Stan Barron was doing sports, but he was also working at the radio station."

"Stan and I had talked before about him hiring me as his second banana. But he was never a staff announcer; he was only a sports guy."

So it was Stan Barron, sports and Rick Azar, weather.

"There was me, Dave Thomas, Bill Gregory, a couple of other guys, and that lasted until 1961, when the best thing that ever happened to me outside of my family happened. That's when Capital Cities bought Channel 7 from Doc Churchill. It was a phenomenal ride after that. "

For the sake of their license, television stations had to run some sort of news program. In the early days of WKBW-TV, even after the 6 o'clock hour had become established as television news time, Channel 7 would run its short news program at 7:20pm, as WGR-TV and WBEN-TV split the 6 o'clock audience between themselves.

And while Irv and KB 1520 were reinventing radio, WKBW-TV's small group of worked-ragged announcers literally didn't compete with the news programs on channels 2 and 4.

The new owners wanted to improve this, but the changes were slow. Since he read the news on Channel 7 regularly at this point, Rick was offered the job of news director.

"When Cap Cities came in," Rick recalls, "they called me into the office, and said, 'would you like to be News Director,' because I had been doing the news at the time."

"I said that would be alright, but I don't want to do the 11 o'clock, because if I'm the News Director, I want to be here at 8 o'clock in the morning. They said we want you to do the 6 and the 11, and I said, well, I don't want to be news director then."

But how about sports director, they asked Rick. "I said to myself, OK, I'll be sports director."

"Bill Gregory was doing the news, I was doing sports, and Dave Thomas would sometimes do weather."

The first piece of the brand that would carry Channel 7 to new astronomic heights was in place.

The next piece would come with a phone call to KB Radio News Director Irv Weinstein, who accepted the long distance charges while he, Elaine, and their children were vacationing in Miami Beach in April, 1964.

"One of the hotel workers came over to us, and said, phone call for Mr. Weinstein. It was Bob King, then the General Manager of television. He asked, 'Irv, how would you like to pick up your stuff and move across the alley to television?'"

For Irv, the call came at just the right time.

"I said, 'Great. Terrific. Wonderful.' And at that point of my career, I was about ready to begin looking again, because frankly, I was getting bored doing pretty much the same thing every day."

"I didn't think I could do much more journalistically on radio at that point, so I thought that television would be a real challenge."

It was a challenge on multiple levels. Aside from setting up camera shots and hitting buttons as a director, Irv had no experience in technically producing a television broadcast.

Buffalo State College Courier Express Collection/Staffannouncer Archives

That, and as Irv first realized as a young man looking for fame and fortune in Hollywood, he didn't exactly have the swashbuckling good looks of a matinee idol.

Rick knew Irv from radio, but even he couldn't be sure that this kid with glasses from Rochester, who'd already been doing the occasional piece of TV, was the answer to any of 7's problems.

"People in the Buffalo broadcast community have always told me I have a great face for radio, and that's true," says Irv.

"If you talk to any of the broadcast consultants, my name would not leap to mind as being an ideal television anchor person. I was short, overweight, had a terminal case of acne."

Powder and lights helped take care of that some, but there was one aspect of television that good lighting and pancake makeup couldn't help: Terror at the sight of the red tally light atop the studio camera.

"The first newscast I did solo, I was terrified. I was petrified. I thought I was going to have a heart attack," Irv remembers. "It was like I had never been on the air. The first television newscast I did, I started getting head tremors, it was just awful. I didn't think I would get through it. In point of fact, this went on for a few months, until I got more comfortable."

"I wasn't comfortable at first, because I couldn't do the things I was famous, *or infamous,* for on radio. There are a lot of things you just can't get away with on television. Even Paul Harvey learned that when he did some television. He's famous for his pauses; well you can't just sit there and not say anything on television. I had to develop an altered style from radio, and that was tough."

"There was no teleprompter in those days; you were looking up and down, and I was doing radio news on television in the beginning. It just didn't work. I looked at some tapes, and I just looked hyper. It was pretty fast paced, so I had to pull back considerably on the pace. I had to pull back on the writing."

So Irv was not an instant success at Channel 7. And for a while, despite being brought over as news director, he wasn't even the top banana. He was *the other guy* on what was then a two anchor news show.

Bill Gregory was Channel 7's top anchor, molded in the fashion of a 1950's announcer. He'd been with the station since day one, and had started his broadcasting career at WGR Radio in 1935, served in World War II and Korea, and had worked at WBUF-TV as well.

He read the news with a big voice, and a nice tone, but was certainly a little cold and stiff by today's standards.

Says Irv of Gregory, "He did a good job, had good pipes, read the words well, but that's pretty much all he did. My job was to write

Buffalo State College Courier Express Collection/Staffannouncer Archives

scripts for him, as well as myself, and we co-anchored the early newscasts."

But Gregory was exactly the kind of announcer that Irv was making mincemeat out of as competition at KB Radio. It wasn't long before the two clashed.

"I wrote something for Bill once, one of my typically slightly outrageous stories, and he says to me, 'I'm not going to read that.'

"'Really, Why not?", Irv asked. "The station manager, he says, wouldn't like it."

"Well, I'm furious at this point. I'm doing all the writing. I'm the news director, and I'm the co-anchor. But, I told him, fine, don't read it; I will. And I'll talk to Bob King about it after the show. He wasn't going to read it, and I wasn't going to argue with him."

"So the next day, I marched into the program director's office. Red Koch, a good guy. I said, 'OK, Red, you have one of the biggest decisions of your day right now. Either me or Gregory.'"

"I explained it to him; he refused to read this story. I'm fine with it; I can get another radio job," Irv told Koch.

Within a week, Gregory was gone, realizing they weren't going anywhere with him.

As someone new to television, who only months before was suffering from "head tremors" as he tried to read the news, Irv knew it was a risk to make such demands, but a risk he had to take.

"I put it on the line. I had three children at home, but I felt pretty secure. I had a proven record, and Gregory didn't. And he was gone."

With Bill Gregory off to his decades-long career in Philadelphia television and radio, it was left to Irv and a skeleton crew crafting the earliest version of *Eyewitness News*.

"We had three people in the news department, myself and two cameramen, Sammy Brunetto and Paul Thomson. We had no budget. For visuals, we'd take the colored section from *The Buffalo Evening News* on Sunday, cut the pictures out, and glue them to cardboard; and we had the chutzpah to call this *Eyewitness News*. But we were very enterprising in the beginning."

And still keep in mind, this wasn't exactly the Irv we've come to know and love just yet.

"I'd say it took me a year to find my persona on the air, during which time, our audience numbers, if they increased at all, it was slight. We weren't making any progress."

"Early on, I was concerned, but really, people accepted me into their hearts and homes. I always had a good language facility, and I knew I'd need it, when I ran across one of the early newscasts at KB Radio that included *Our Lady of Czestochowa*. I hit that cold. I have no idea to this day what I actually said on the air. But I learned quickly."

Buffalo State College Courier Express Collection/Staffannouncer Archives

"We had no ratings in the beginning, we tried everything. We danced out in front of the station. We gave away green stamps," says Irv with only moderate exaggeration.

Irv was brought to Channel 7 to put together something all together different from what people were used to seeing on Buffalo television.

"We had to define ourselves as being a different news program," said Irv. "Part of that was related to the chemistry between Rick Azar, Tom Jolls, and myself; and the other part, was in the approach to writing the story. I realized, early in the game, if we did the same kind of news program as Channels 2 and 4, we weren't going anywhere."

After about a year of Irv getting more comfortable with television, and Irv and Rick were starting to find a rapport with one another, one more addition was made to the team that would dominate Buffalo television news for the next quarter century.

By 1965, Tom Jolls had been anchoring the nightly 11 o'clock news on Channel 4 seven nights a week, but he was still one of the more junior members of WBEN's staff of well-over a dozen announcers.

"Tom was the last plug," says Rick. "Bob King, the general manager, was looking to put someone permanently on the weather. It was a revolving door there for a while."

"They had their eye on Tom, he came on board, and it was a ride after that."

Walking into Channel 7, Tom didn't know Irv, but he did know Rick, back in the days when Tom was still a high school kid and Rick was working his way through college.

"He worked in Lockport when he was very young, and I was very young," says Tom. "I was 14 or 15, and he was one of the first announcers at the Lockport station in 1948 or 49 at WUSJ."

It's part of the background of the Irv, Rick, and Tom story that makes it all so unique.

Buffalo State College Courier Express Collection/Staffannouncer Archives

"His name was Rick Corey in those days," remembers Tom, "who, again, remembers watching the man he'd come to eat dinner with at least 3 nights a week, thinking, "Oh boy, how lucky he is. I wish I could do something like that some day."

The longest running anchor team in history had been put together. But for Tom, at this point, it was more about weekends off than the annals of broadcasting legend. He'd been working 7 days a week at WBEN-TV when the call came from KB-TV.

"The three of us were put together with a plan, I guess, but I didn't know there was a plan at the time. Program Director Lyle "Red" Koch could foresee that Rick and Irv and me would make a great team. What he foresaw, I don't know how he came about it, but he thought this would really work out."

Irv looks back at it this way.

"So they got these three guys together. One guy who bears a vague resemblance to Rudolph Valentino and you've got Truman Goodheart here from Lockport, every mother's son, standing up for the American *way of life*, the flag, and apple pie."

"Then they've got this vertically challenged guy with a 1940's haircut and a terrible complexion. And nobody believed, *not even us,* that the audience was going to accept us. Fortunately, it did."

But as *Rudolph Valentino* at the sports desk and *Truman Goodheart* on the weather outside readily admit, it was that *ethnic type* with bad skin reading the news who was *the glue* holding the whole thing together.

"Irv was the adhesive that held us together," says Tom. "He could come out with the funniest things, and I never knew what he was going to say to me, or what the reaction would be."

Tom didn't know, Rick didn't know, and the viewers didn't know. That's what made this newscast different from anything else that had ever been seen in Buffalo, or anywhere, for that matter.

"When Rick, Tom and I were first teamed by General Manager Bob King and Program Director Red Koch, it was a time when news was not valued that greatly," Irv recalls. "It was a requirement of the FCC; if you didn't have news, they'd pull your license, so they didn't care much what the hell we did."

But what the staff at Channel 7 did, lead by Irv, was creating a product *so different* from anything *not only* in Buffalo, but so different from anything anywhere in the country, that people couldn't help but talk about it and tune in.

"When Irv started to poke fun at me or he would make some funny comment, people loved that. People loved it, because this had never been done before," says Tom with a smile. "Certainly they didn't get at at 'BEN, you didn't get at WGR in those days, though eventually they tried to emulate us."

Will success spoil Weinstein, Azar & Jolls? We don't think so. They're the most popular television news team in town because of their warm, friendly, human style of reporting. They're not afraid to smile or even poke fun at each other once in a while . . . . all done without taking the accuracy and seriousness out of the news. Will success spoil Weinstein, Azar and Jolls? Watch them and see what you think!

Eyewitness News/6 and 11 PM WKBW-TV 7

Buffalo State College Courier Express Collection/Staffannouncer Archives

"I didn't see anything particularly special about it," admits Tom, "but when we started to see the ratings start to change, management was silently smiling to themselves saying, 'I think we've got it here!'"

A big part of what made that work, especially in a place like Buffalo, was that while some of the stories and the writing may have been flashy, the personalities were more Main Street than Hollywood. "One of the reasons for our success, one of the reasons that people took to the three of us, is that we are regular people," says Irv. "They sense that we were approachable; we were the people who lived next door. The sense is that we are the type of people who won't be appearing on the cover of the *National Enquirer*."

"Part of our success was, that we didn't know we were being successful, didn't know we were having that kind of success," says Rick. "Not from that point of view of where there are a lot of people in the business who want to play star, and want to be a star.... 'Look at me, I'm on TV.' We never had that feeling. The only reason we felt we were successful is because we worked our asses off. That's what we did. We were bound and determined to be the best that we could be, and I think that paid off. None of us ever felt, 'Gee, we're better than the other guys.' No, no, no. We just worked harder than the other guys, and that's why we were successful."

"We came across as the guy next door," adds Tom. "In fact, Hal Crowther at the News said I was looked upon as 'every mother's son.' But how all that comes across, how it's all perceived, you're just lucky that that's the way it works. We didn't go at it any special way. I didn't try to be that. It just happened. I have always just been me. I don't think I changed any from when I started out, back at the 250 watter (radio station) in Lockport. I don't think I ever did anything different."

That sense, emphasized by each of the stars of the show, was more than just a show business front.

"All of us are married to our first wives," says Irv. "We've gone to each other's children's happy occasions: weddings, bar mitzvahs, bat mitzvahs."

"It was a very unusual melting pot for the three of us," says Rick.

So close at work, it had to spill over a little. Rick says, "The three of us were very close in the work arena, in the work place. Tom would

Buffalo State College Courier Express Collection/Staffannouncer Archives

hangout in one of two places, either in Irv's office, or my office. We got very close that way."

"Once in a while Irv and I would go to the movies, Tom and I would go to a greasy spoon on Niagara Street 3 nights a week, a place Irv wouldn't be caught dead in," Rick said with a smile.

"Every Monday, at 3 o'clock, Irv and I would be either in my office or his office, and we'd sit there and talk family stuff. How's Elaine? How's Edith? How are the kids? We'd also talk life stuff. Did you see this movie? See this play? It was the same thing with Tom. That was our social life. It occurred while we were working."

"We all knew each other, our families knew each other, our wives knew each other, all that kind of stuff; but it wasn't like we were getting together outside of the work place."

But, Rick says, that was good enough.

"The workplace was incredible for the three of us. It made us close. We were so close to one another, we felt like we could say whatever we wanted to one another. We used to tease the heck out of Tom," says Rick laughing with the kind of laugh that comes when there's a good story that can't be told.

"I don't know," Rick says, "it was almost family."

The newsman takes it half a step further. Irv says, "We were lucky. We had two families. We had our families at home, and we had each other. Irv, Rick, Tom. We truly love each other."

Like any family, many of the best times come at the expense of one another.

It's an indelible image in the minds of thousands of Buffalonians of three or four different generations: Tom Jolls says, "Back inside to you, Irv." Irv cracks a joke about Tom, his forecast, or his clothes. As you see Irv and Tom on the screen at the same time for a few moments, you hear Irv's joke, often accompanied by a devilish grin, and Tom's glowing eyes and laughter at whatever mischievous verbal shot was just taken.

No one ever mistook what was going on there.

"Everyone always saw through it," says Tom, "That it was all just in good fun," even when the handiwork of Mrs. Jolls was involved.

"For a while, my wife was making my suits for me, and I just had some sort of a strange attraction to something different," remembers Tom.

"Something flamboyant in a way; but not too far out. That kind of got attached to me, 'How many sports coats does he have?' I had a few, but I really enjoying doing something I figured people would get a kick out of it; 'What's he wearing tonight?' It worked for me."

And worked for Irv's one liners, too.

"Irv just had that ability, that quick wit about him," says Tom. "Rick too, had a quick wit. I was kind of just there. I don't know what I contributed to what was going on. It was just fun being a part of it. I never took offense at it, because I always knew where it was coming from, no matter what he would say, or how it might seem."

One place where Irv found himself on the other side of it was when Rick would set him up as the all-knowing sports soothsayer, when it couldn't have been further from the truth.

"Rick recognized very early on that I didn't know anything about sports," Irv can admit now with a devilish grin. "I didn't know anything about it in '64; I didn't know anything about in '98 when I left.

"He would kid me about that, not necessarily on the air, but occasionally; particularly when I'd try to make a prediction about how the Bills were going to do. I had no idea, but I knew that people were curious about what I thought about the team, even though I just didn't have any idea."

Buffalo State College Courier Express Collection/Staffannouncer Archives

The viewers of Western New York liked these guys, and were interested in what they had to say, and the completely different way in which they were saying it.

"That is, in addition to the *who, what, where, when and why* of the story," says Irv, "adding some of the emotional sense of what you were talking about."

Eyewitness News was able to tap into the psyche of Buffalo in a way that had never been done before; by creating news for people who weren't used to having news tailored to them.

"It helped that I grew up in a multi-ethnic neighborhood in Rochester. Italian, Polish, German, Jewish. Reading Polish is like any other language; you learn the basic rules, and you get by."

And just the fact that someone cared enough to know started giving Channel 7 viewers who felt they weren't even on the radar at other stations.

"I think I had a lot of credibility. I think I projected believability. Credibility, believability, whatever you want to call it, at the heart of the matter, that's all you're selling-- Do people believe what it is that you're telling them. "

But even with this idea, this theory on how to present a completely different and at the same time captivating and wildly popular news show was completely unproven.

Plenty of hard work, over a number of years, went into building *Eyewitness News* from a 7pm non-competitor to a Queen City institution.

"It was not a simple process," remembers Irv well. "It took us about 7 years to go from number 3 to number 1. I would say, by the late 1960s, we were making pretty big gains in the numbers."

"It wasn't necessarily an anti-anything. We were trying to be proactive about defining our news program as much as possible from the other

Buffalo State College Courier Express Collection/Staffannouncer Archives

Buffalo State College Courier Express Collection/Staffannouncer Archives

stations in town. When people went across that dial, we wanted them to know when they hit us. They didn't even need to see the anchor person. They could see a few seconds of the story and they knew where they were on the television dial, because of the way the story was being reported.

No matter how good or interesting *Eyewitness News* was, there were still major circumstances over which Irv, Rick, and Tom had no control. Like the availability of the *remote* control.

"Channel 2 benefitted tremendously from the fact that *The Tonight Show* followed their show. People didn't want to get up to change the channel after the news to watch Johnny Carson. That's not to cast aspersions on Channel 2. They did a fine job; but they benefited from the fact that the number one late night show followed them.

"Conversely, when I started at Channel 7, ABC was running programs like *My Mother the Car*. We had no network support at all. So whatever we did, the achievement was the achievement of the team. And I don't just mean the anchor team, I mean reporters, producers, writers, management. You really need management support to do some of the things that were a little off center."

By late 1967, Eyewitness News was going head to head against channels 2 and 4 with a 6 o'clock newscast.

"One of the things that really helped us was Channel 4, to their everlasting credit, ignored us. We were 'just those guys over on Main Street.' They weren't worried about us, because they were the source for *responsible* news… and that was *fine*… that was *perfect*. They helped us."

For the first 20 years Channel 4 was on the air, though its newscasts were the most watched, the men who delivered the news were not necessarily trained journalists. They were announcers who read scripts, often prepared by newspaper reporters from the Buffalo Evening News.

Buffalo State College Courier Express Collection/Staffannouncer Archives

As WGR-TV 2 turned to the cocky and flamboyant Ron Hunter in an attempt to "out-Irv" Irv in the early 70s, WBEN-TV hired longtime CBS Washington Correspondent Stephen Rowan as Channel 4's evening news anchor to bring a strong journalistic presence to its newscast.

"They ran all these promos, that Walter Cronkite Loves Steve Rowan, and they went to an hour of news at Channel 4. They went to an hour. This was a big move, the first hour long newscast in Buffalo, and this was going to show everyone that they were the guys with the firepower," Irv remembers.

"We watched it very closely, and we loved it, because what they were doing was taking an hour to do a *half hour* of news. An interview that would normally last 2 minutes; it would last 5 minutes."

"We actually ran a promo that said, '*Eyewitness News...* All the news... *in half the time.*'"

Creative and catchy promotional announcements were only part of the *Eyewitness News* approach. There were many creative, innovative, borderline kitschy and mostly 'borrowed' elements that made Channel 7's newscast stand out. Irv remembers the origins of a few, like the *Eyewitness News Reel.*

A staple of movie going in the 40s, and 50s was the RKO-Pathe newsreels, which opened with a few moments of bright and brassy music and a rooster crowing, and there were similarly produced newsreels with Ed Herlihy narrating, as Irv says, "How the boys are doing 'over there.'"

"Basically, that was the whole idea of the *Eyewitness News Reel*. That's it. I'd love to tell you that it was one of my brilliant ideas, but that's not true. (Channel 7 General Manager) Bob King came back from a business trip where he saw this on a station somewhere else in the country. He explained, 'Just like the old newsreels, short stories, 20 seconds long. Maybe this is something you could do, Irv.' In a blinding flash of intelligence, it came to me that that is a *great* idea."

"It's a wonderful vehicle to get through a lot of different stories, to load your newscast up. We would have newscasts with 20 or 30 different stories. We'd score the stories with music, and title cards."

"This is very important. Maybe not to the general audience, but to me. When they heard that music come on, *fire music*, for example. They could be down in the cellar or out in the yard, and they'd race into the living room to see the blaze. They knew something important was happening. It was almost Pavlovian."

"It's all a part of that old saw, 'You have to get their attention before you can give them information.'"

Eyewitness News cameras would show up to dozens of meetings and events, and people would see 15 seconds worth of their event on the news that night, often in that *Eyewitness News Reel*.

"It meant a lot to them. It meant the world to them. It meant that Channel 7 is not just a television station, but it's a part of the same community they are a part of. "

It was Tom Jolls' voice you heard, not Irv's, on that Eyewitness News Reel for all those years. The writing, though, was all Irv all the way. Occasionally, that led to a scene almost worthy of the newsreel itself.

"We always had time to rehearse, so I would go in the newsroom, and watch the film clips as they ran through the old reel to reel projectors," remembers Tom.

"One night, I didn't have a chance to rehearse, and I came across a word; I saw it coming up in the script, and I didn't know what it was, didn't know what it meant. I'd never heard the word before... fiat."

Before the Italian car became more of a household name, *fiat* meant an order, or a decree. But it may as well have been Greek to Tom that night.

"I'm saying to myself as I approach it, 'What is this?, What does this word mean?, Is it a typo?, How do I say it?"

Tom Jolls Collection/Staffannouncer Archives

Not sure of himself, he skipped it when he hit it live.

"It changed the whole meaning of the story, and boy, did I hear about it from Irv," Tom remembers with his usual smile. "He was furious, and he really should have been. My only defense though, was I didn't have a chance to rehearse this, and I didn't know what it meant."

Just as the newsreel was a borrowed element, so too, were *Eyewitness News* standards like Tom Jolls nightly reminder, "It's 11 o'clock. Do you know where your children are?"

"Again an out of town import," admits Irv. "There are almost no original ideas having to do with almost anything."

Another borrowed element: The famous *Eyewitness News Theme.*

Believe it or not, the song, "Move Closer To Your World," written by Al Ham, actually has lyrics known in several media markets around the country, most notably Philadelphia, where the song had endured as well as it has in Buffalo.

It was, of course, the melding of the incredibly original elements, and the incredible borrowed elements that helped make *Eyewitness News* (a borrowed name) an enduring institution.

Of course, it goes without saying, taking a jumble of good ideas, fast moving pictures, and alliterative writing does not always make for a popular or successful, let alone legendary newscast.

In 1977, WNED-TV, Buffalo's public broadcaster, produced a documentary called *The Battle to Win 6 & 11*, focused on Buffalo's local newscasts. Right at the apex of his popularity, Irv explained to the PBS cameras how and why *Eyewitness News* was so successful.

Let me say with as much humility as I can muster...

The success of every news program is dependent to a very great extent on how well the anchorman or woman communicates with the audience.

Buffalo State College Courier Express Collection/Staffannouncer Archives

the
(W)EINSTEIN THEORY

To Irv Weinstein, WKBW-TV News Director, effective broadcast journalism means accurate reporting, combined with the best on-location news film. It means warm and friendly people like the Eyewitness News team who have been around long enough to really understand what's important to Western New Yorkers. It means communicating better than anybody else.

And here's the proof that the Weinstein Theory works! The latest 1973 Nielsen Audience Survey shows that **more people in Western New York watch Eyewitness News at both 6 & 11 p.m. than any other newscast.** Test the Weinstein Theory yourself, we think you'll agree that it's pure genius!

*Nielsen Station Index, Feb.-March, 1973. Subject to qualifications.

EYEWITNESS NEWS · 6 & 11PM · WKBW-TV

Buffalo State College Courier Express Collection/Staffannouncer Archives

I think we have been relatively successful in this regard. I think one of the things that has worked for us is longevity.

I have been on the air in this market for about 18 years. I'm a known quantity. Irv Weinstein, is, to many people, a guy they know, perhaps like, and feel comfortable with, and trust.

That is something you build up over a long period of time; the kind of thing no amount of promotion or publicity can achieve. If a new guy comes into the market, as has happened over the last few years, you can promote him as the greatest thing since rubber bands. But if the audience looks in, and they don't perceive that he is what you tell them he is, they'll not only not turn you back again, but they will get angry, because, in fact, you lied to them.

When I took over television in 1964, I like to describe our ratings as number 4 in a three station market.

I can't recall exactly what the numbers were, but suffice it to say, that the sermonette, shortly before sign-off, was doing better in the ratings than our news.

I sat back and watched what the other two stations were doing in town, and they were doing a good job, but they were essentially doing the same thing; taking a relatively conservative approach to news presentation.

We began by taking a more aggressive approach to local news coverage. We decided at the outset, that what people were really interested in, in a local news program, was 'local news.'

We knew we were dealing with a medium which is a visual medium, and therefore we decided to make our news program as highly visual as possible. Our writing style was, and is, I think, more aggressive than any other news operation, not only in this area, but probably in the country. We have a very unique approach to communicating information through words and pictures.

Then, of course, there are our on-air people, both reporters and our anchor people. Rick, Tom, and myself have been together from almost the start. I think we work well as a team, I think the acceptance from the audience has shown that we wear well, kind of like a good worsted suit.

There's always a problem you run into in this business of running stale, because your audience is changing, your demographics are changing. But I think we've done a good job of staying fresh. I think we've managed to keep our individual styles fresh. Maybe a few more gray hairs, but I don't think anyone thinks of us as old fogies.

It took us about two years before we started to move the numbers. Once we started to move the numbers, every rating book showed an increase of at least a point or two. It was slow. Painfully slow.

We did some good on-air promotion, and some folks began to say, 'Hey, these guys are doing something different; giving us a viable option to what the other guys are doing.' So they looked in, and they liked what they saw. They told their friends, and they looked in. It had a snowballing effect.

By 1967 and 1968, we were doing well. Very well. By 1972, we were dominant, and have remained so. We're probably the highest rated ABC affiliate in the country. It probably helped us to some extent that our competition didn't adjust to the new competitive situation. In other words, we were the young kids on the block, and they ignored us. That is, until suddenly, naked terror appeared at the other shops when they realized we had suddenly pulled ahead of them. It came as a great surprise to some people, I think. They really helped us, I think, by not doing anything different than what they had already been doing.

As the long time boss at Channel 7, Phil Beuth acknowledges that he, and even *Mickey Mouse*, owe a great deal to Buffalo's favorite anchor team.

"Their record is phenomenal. Almost 25 years together, unparalleled in the history of television. As their boss for 11 years, I can add something you don't know about them.

"WKBW-TV sent a lot of money to Capital Cities (*the station's corporate owners*). In the early years, Channel 7 added mightily to the growth of the company. The ratings success of Eyewitness News with Irv, Rick and Tom, was so important to the growth and financial health of Capital Cities, and helped lead to the tremendous growth of the company's stock."

Irv, Tom, Rick, and longtime Channel 7 GM Phil Beuth
Irv Weinstein Collection/Staffannouncer Archives

Capital Cities Communications still owned Channel 7 when it purchased ABC-TV for $3.5 billion in 1985. And although Channel 7 was sold off in 1986, many long time employees still owned Cap Cities stock when Disney bought Cap Cities/ABC in 1996.

Beuth continued, "The ratings success was undeniably amazing. For many years, the 6 and 11 o'clock newscast's shares were the highest in any three station market in the country for 7 or 8 years in a row."

"(Their) work, personality, mutual respect, and personality made them welcome members of the family in homes around WNY."

The phenomenal ride of Eyewitness News, combined with the phenomenal ride of Capital Cities, insured that unlike many (even great) local news broadcasters, neither Irv, nor Rick, nor Tom would have to worry about the material things of life. Like many of their WKBW-TV brethren, each was guaranteed financial comfort with stock options and a great employer.

Chapter 6: Topping Tonight's Eyewitness News...

Taking vacations into account, Irv uttered the phrase "Topping tonight's *Eyewitness News*" upwards of 17,000 times over 34 years to open a newscast. Add in Rick's 13,000 sportscasts and 500 play-by-play jobs, plus Tom's 17,000 weather outside segments and 5,500 episodes of the Commander Tom Show, and the raw numbers are staggering.

With an average of 25 news stories per newscast, that's 425,000 stories, give or take 25,000, which Irv Weinstein shared with us on Channel 7. Half a million stories.

 While hundreds of those stories may have involved animals trained to be engaged in some sort of unusual activity, like water skiing squirrels, skateboard riding bulldogs, or a shoe-shining monkey; many thousands more are the stories that have changed the way we live.

It's an easy question to ask a newsman who'd been at it as long as Irv.

 "Which story affected you most?"

For Irv, that story happened about 6 months before his famed television career began, as a newsman at KB Radio. It was a typical gray November afternoon in 1963, and Irv was ensconced inside the KB Radio newsroom at the station's Main Street studios.

"Suddenly, the *Associated Press* wires started clacking away. Not printing anything, just clacking away. I looked at the wire, and there were just three words on the paper when it finally started printing, it said: KENNEDY SHOT DALLAS."

"It was unbelievable. We just couldn't believe what was happening. And then when the word came, that the President had in fact died, everyone just started sobbing."

"All of the sudden, KB Radio went from a Top 40 format, to playing music that sounded like it came from a funeral parlor."

"I've been asked what story affected you the most. That one, and not just me, anyone who was in broadcasting, including normally rock-solid-steel Walter Cronkite. *Everyone* was crying. It was a terrible, terrible, terrible time."

Men on the Moon

One of the reasons Kennedy was so well loved, was that he made America excited about its future. He said by the end of the decade, man would walk on the moon, and on July 20, 1969, he was proved prophetic.

Apollo 11 landed on the lunar surface, and Neil Armstrong spoke of his "one small step for man, one giant leap for mankind."

"I still cannot believe that there was a man on the moon," says Irv. "I look up at that thing at night and I see what most people imagine: the man on the moon; the face with dots for eyes and a little mouth. When those words were spoken, it was absolutely incredible that one of us was on the moon."

Priest Murders

In 1987, Buffalo spent a fortnight in fear as two Catholic priests, Msgr. David P. Herlihy and Fr. A. Joseph Bissonette, were killed two weeks apart inside the rectories of their East Side parishes.

Each man was tied to a chair, stabbed, and bludgeoned to death; and in each case the home was ransacked and robbed.

Two teens, one of whom knew the priests, were arrested and confessed to the murders.

Irv says this story very deeply touched him and the viewers. "Every murder is a tragedy, but somehow when it happens to clergymen, men of God, men of peace, I think it had a particularly powerful impact on the people in this area."

Propane Explosion

Two days after Christmas in 1983, five firefighters from Ladder 5 and two civilians were killed when an illegal 500 pound propane tank

Buffalo State College Courier Express Collection/Staffannouncer Archives

exploded in a warehouse at North Division and Grosvenor Streets downtown.

"The blast rocked an entire Buffalo neighborhood, destroying homes, upending a fire engine, and killing 5 firemen," Irv recalls. "Probably the most memorable and tragic fire the city has suffered."

The firefighters were responding to reports of a leak, when that leak ignited. The blast could be felt miles away, but most everyone was touched by the heart wrenching emotion of the story.

"It was just awful to watch not just for our audience, but as we were reporting it. The people who shot the video. How could they not be affected by seeing these people dedicated to saving lives; having their own lives taken so quickly and so violently."

19 other firefighters were injured in the blast, and Sheehan Memorial Hospital treated over 70 people injured in the blast.

Bethlehem Steel furnaces go cold
A story 12 years in the making, Bethlehem Steel began its gradual shutdown in 1971, as half of the company's 18,000 plant workers were laid off.

At the height of production in Lackawanna in 1965, Bethlehem employed 20,000 workers. 18 years later, in 1983, all but a few hundred of the remaining 8,000 were given pink slips.

Irv calls it "an American tragedy," and, "the most cataclysmic economic event in the modern history of this area."

Return to Auschwitz
The most infamous and deadly of 6 Nazi death camps located inside occupied Poland in World War II, current estimates are that 1.1 million people died at Auschwitz, 90 percent of them Jews.

Unlike coverage of breaking news stories and events, bringing Buffalo the story of the horror of the concentration camp was not aided by the adrenaline of getting the developing news on the air, and trying, to some degree, to suppress the revulsion of it all in an effort to get the facts across.

The story at Auschwitz *is* evil, those who succumbed to evil, and the few who overcame it.

"Going to Auschwitz, was the singular event, not just in my professional life, but in my personal life. The feeling, as you walk through that camp, with the knowledge of what went on there, is just unimaginable. If this had happened in the 10th century, it would be incredible. But the fact that it happened in the middle of the 20th century, makes it even more incredible."

While the news is obviously the story of our lives, the ups and downs of our Buffalo sports teams might be the stories of our collective souls to one degree or another. Rick Azar was one of us, the smart guy on the barstool telling us from a great vantage point—from the inside—what was going on with the Bills, the Sabres, the Braves, Little 3 Basketball, Wrestling at the Aud. He was the public-at-large's direct connection to the sports of a simpler time.

Over the years, Rick has talked publicly and at length about his memories of sporting events and figures. Most of the stories that follow come from a series of roundtable discussions with WNSA Radio about Buffalo's sports history in 2001.

Professional Wrestling
"My uncle used to take me down to the Broadway Auditorium to watch professional wrestlers like Frank Sexton, The French Angel, Whipper Billy Watson, and Iron Talon, who used to ride around on a 10 speed bike. I could go on and on about those guys and how good they were."

"Whipper Billy and Frank Sexton were in this big match, and Whipper Billy had Sexton in one hold for 15 minutes. Can you imagine sitting today, at a professional wrestling match, watching something like that? You'd be surprised the tension that was built up by that. The fans, they were sitting on the edge of their seats. Wondering who would give up first, and it was legit, because his arm was white when he left go."

"That all changed when along came a guy named Gorgeous George. He changed the face of pro wrestling forever. It was a good PR move, it was a big uplift, but that was the start of the unfortunate thing that pro wrestling's turned into today."

"I did a half hour show with the wrestlers at the Aud once a week, and one time, Bruno Sammartino did 20 pushups with me sitting on his shoulder. I challenged him, said, you can't do that. We did it right there on television."

"And you can't talk about wrestling in Buffalo without mentioning Ilio DiPaolo. He came here from Italy via Argentina, and made a big impact on this community on so many levels." A big man with an even bigger heart, who chose Buffalo and changed the city for the better.

let's get our heads together

Iroquois

HAVE ONE WITH RICK AZAR

Little 3 Basketball
"Those schools were major entities back in those days. You were able to get a Calvin Murphy to go to Niagara or a Bob Lanier to go to St. Bonaventure. You can't get those players anymore, because those sorts of players (both from Buffalo, both now in the Basketball Hall of Fame) are going to more glamorous schools, schools that weren't involved in basketball back in those days."

"Now, when you ask a young man to come to Canisius instead of UCLA, it's kind of a tough sell. That's one of the things that's changed. And in those days, all of the broadcast rights were with the local stations. There were no network agreements, no cable."

"Even back before 1950, teams would book here at the old Auditorium on their way to Madison Square Garden, or on their way back from New York. Buffalo was a big train stop. You might see Utah playing Wyoming as the first game of a doubleheader at the Aud. Obviously, that's never going to happen again."

"They were great days, but I think now the schools are representing themselves fairly well. There are a lot of NCAA teams at that level now. Once in a while you get one to go all the way to the semis in the tournament. That's something to hope for, but to lament, to hope to get that back, it's wasting a lot of time."

Randy Smith
A soccer and basketball player from Long Island, Smith went to Buffalo State, and then was drafted in the NBA by the Buffalo Braves, only to go on to become the NBA's Iron Man, playing in 906 straight games from 1972-82.

"He could run faster, dribbling a basketball, than most men could run without dribbling a basketball. He was something very special."

Bob McAdoo
Drafted by the Braves in 1972, he was the 1973 NBA Rookie of the year, and the league's MVP in 1975.

Buffalo State College Courier Express Collection/Staffannouncer Archives

"He was the best pure shooter I ever saw in basketball. If he had a shot, from just about anywhere on the court, nine times out of ten, it was in the hoop. A pure, pure shooter. There were some other things he didn't do as well, like he always wanted the ball. If you passed it into him, you never got it back. But it was an amazing thing to watch him shoot. He was great. There is no doubt about that."

Wayne Gretzky

"Gretzky and the Oilers were spending about three days in Western New York on an eastern swing, and I had never seen so many guys at practice at Sabreland. There were usually three, maybe four reporters tops. There must have been 25 or 30 guys out there. We set up a press conference for Wayne, so we all get our cameras ready, and Wayne walks over to where we've all set up. He walks right up to me, with everyone else all around and says, 'My mother told me not to come home from Buffalo without your autograph.' I said, 'Hunh?!?' The Gretzkys used to watch us on TV all the time in Brantford, Ontario. For as many autographs as he's signed, I wonder how many he's asked for?"

"That's the highlight of my career!"

Joe Namath

"Another highlight of my career: One time Joe and I were on the golf course down some place warm, and these guys are looking at us once, then again, from across the course. Then, they started walking over, and Joe's probably thinking, 'Oh, boy, here we go.'"

"Well they walk right past Namath and say, 'Hey, aren't you Rick Azar? We love you and Irv.' Another career highlight."

Howard Cosell

"When Monday Night Football came to town, they had a special luncheon for him, and told me I was going to be the MC. I said, 'Please! Find someone else!' I was afraid Howard was going to destroy me. I was making calls to people asking what I should say, what shouldn't I say."

"But Cosell was a very insightful individual. Not the world's most charming man by any stretch of the imagination, but, fortunately, I happen to get along with him fairly well. He didn't like too many people in any of the media. Very few in TV, even fewer writers."

"One guy he liked was Will McDonough from the Boston Globe. We'd be in public, and Howard would make a show saying, 'This is the only writer in America who knows anything about professional football.' I don't know how much Howard Cosell knew about professional football."

Lou Saban
"I was doing post game interviews in this little room with a small couch after another Bills loss to the Dolphins, and Lou Saban comes in a huff, plops down on the seat, and he's shaking his head. Those of us who knew Saban knew something was going on. I asked him a couple of questions, and he just started repeating himself, 'I don't know what I'm gonna do. I don't believe it. I don't know if I can handle it.'"

"John Leypoldt missed a field goal, and he took it personally. 'How could he do this to me?'"

"I'm saying to myself, this guy is going to quit his job on the air, right here. Essentially, he did quit. Two weeks later, he left."

"He did that the first time he quit as Bills coach, too. The Bills had just won a second AFL Championship, and he came into the announce booth at Channel 7, sat down in the chair, and said to me, 'Can you believe that guy? All he offered me was a thousand dollar raise.' I said, 'Lou, wait a minute.' He was upset, and he quit that time, too."

Stan Barron
"One of the most dedicated guys I ever knew in the business. And he knew every little detail about pronunciation, rules, this and that, that was him. He loved what he did, and he was good at what he did."

"He would take it personally when the high school teams wouldn't call in their scores, he wanted to put them on the air."

Play WKBW.

For the most exciting radio football coverage you've ever heard.

AL MELTZER   RICK AZAR   EDDIE RUTKOWSKI

GAME DAY

"Bills Replay" 45 minutes before kick off

"Line Up" 15 minutes before kick off

"Game Plan" 5 minutes before kick off

"Bills Scoreboard" Immediately following the final gun

"Bills Locker Room" 5 minutes after the final gun

WEEKLY FEATURES

Nine times every Monday "Monday Quarterback"

Nine times every Thursday "Scouting Report"

Nine times every Saturday "Coaches Report"

**Hear it all on the
50,000 watt flagship station
of the Buffalo Bills
WKBW Radio·1520·Buffalo**

Buffalo State College Courier Express Collection/Staffannouncer Archives

IRV: BUFFALO'S ANCHORMAN!

Ralph Wilson

"I wish somebody could pick apart his brain to see what made him do some of the things he did do, and not do some of the things he should have done. He could be very exasperating. You'd wonder sometimes, how can he be doing this? He was very impulsive; on a lot of occasions I saw him going through that impulsiveness."

"But over and beyond that, you have to look at some of the other things. The fact that he bet on this city, says a lot about the guy. He could have done a lot of other things; he could have gone to a lot of other places. He had other choices, but he came here, and he has stuck it out through thick and thin. I appreciate that about him. He's made plenty of mistakes, but I don't think there's a perfect owner alive, really. I tend more to look at that positive side of Ralph Wilson rather than look at some of the inadequacies that maybe he might have."

"He's been a loyal guy to Buffalo, and I think that's super."

OJ Simpson

While the abhorrent behavior he's displayed over the last two decades have made him a pariah, when he was at the top, there was no greater, more popular Buffalo athlete that Orenthal James Simpson. And there was no Buffalo sportscaster closer to OJ, than Rick Azar.

To look back at one of the more tragic figures in American History is almost impossible. Instead, we roll back the tape of the Bills 1973 highlight reel; as narrated by Rick.

The tape is split in two even parts. The first, talks about the first 13 games of a 14 game season. The second half is all about December 16, 1973. A snowy day at Shea Stadium for the Bills and Jets.

"The Bills narrowly missed the playoffs," Rick says on the tape, "but didn't miss their appointment with professional football destiny."

"A moment of ultimate triumph for Buffalo, and its irresistible force: OJ Simpson. With all eyes in Shea Stadium locked on number 32, OJ set his sights on Jimmy Brown's single season rushing record of 1,863 yards. Early in the first quarter, Simpson reached the threshold."

Rick was in the booth as sports history was twice made that day. First as OJ Simpson broke Jim Brown's record, then as he broke the 2000 yard mark.

The sound bites are famous not only in Buffalo, but are known by NFL fans everywhere.

"Well gentlemen, we are coming upon it. The Juice should break the NFL rushing record in this next series."

"Simpson, running left, Simpson, breaking loose… and there it is…

Eddie Rutkowski, Jeff Kaye, Al Meltzer, and Rick Azar in the booth for Buffalo Bills Football. Staffannouncer Archives

"He did it! Alright! He needed four yards, he got five, and this crowd… the whole team is gathering around him, congratulating him, hitting him on the head, there isn't a person sitting down. Give credit to these Jets fans, they came here to see him break the record. There's no doubt about it. I think the Jets showed up to watch him break the record. Joe Namath said to me on Wednesday, 'Sure I want to see him break the record. He deserves it, he's that kind of a guy. I'm not rooting against my defensive ball players, but he's gotta get it, and he did."

Later in the game, it was history again, as Simpson became the first man to gain 200 yards in a single NFL season.

As his teammates hoisted OJ Simpson onto their shoulders after a 5 or 6 yard gain in the snow, Rick said famously over WKBW Radio, "I just wonder if the three of us at this moment fully realize what has been our great privilege to see and broadcast and account for, every inch of what has happened this season. I don't think it'll hit me for quite a while yet. But it's been a thrill for me, let me tell ya, to watch OJ Simpson run, for 2000 yards, in one season."

Of his 2000 yard season, Rick said in 2002, "It's in the history books, and you're a part of that. Those of us who have been in this business for a lifetime, working hard at our jobs, and doing a good job, never get that opportunity. That never comes their way. Al Meltzer, Eddie Rutkowski and I were very fortunate to have something like that come our way."

"I feel very privileged to have been there, and be part of it."
And at that same time, even long after the murder trial and much of the circus, Rick admitted, "in spite of the problems he has had, I don't think we've ever seen a runner with the ability that he had to run."

Tough Guy or Nice Guy?
One of the more popular series of promos involving Rick Azar involved the argument over whether he was a tough guy or a nice guy; or whether he was a nice tough guy or a tough nice guy.

So, to end that argument which started in a bakery in a TV promo 30 years ago, which is it, Rick?

"I like to hope that I'm a nice guy," says Rick, "but that's not for me to judge. Being a tough guy, I suppose I could make that judgment better than the other."

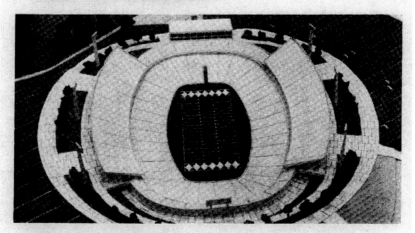
Buffalo State College Courier Express Collection/Staffannouncer Archives

And in retrospect, Rick says he must have been tough to do some of the things and say some of the things he said over the years, especially in his opinion pieces during Eyewitness Sports.

"I've taken on some things that I think about now, and I think, 'How the hell did I even have the balls to say that on the air… Not that I regret it, because I strongly believed everything I said on the air."

Weather really should be first. Even though Tom's 7 day Accu Weather forecast was always dead last on Eyewitness News, for better or for worse, it's what Buffalo is known for. And I'm not talking about our beautiful summers. Snow. And the national attention about our snow, and Johnny Carson's jokes about our snow started with one raging, hellish nightmare of a snow storm we've never since seen anything even remotely close to: The Blizzard.

Sure, there's a year that goes along with that title, but when you say emphatically, 'the Blizzard,' there's only one you can mean. It's the same storm you can thank whenever someone asks you in August if all the snow's melted yet.

Blizzard of '77
"It was a corker," Irv says in an uncharacteristically understated manner.

Temperatures were below normal temperatures for the months leading up to the storm. Powdery snow had been piling up on an early-frozen Lake Erie. Then more snow and winds clocked to 69 miles an hour from January 28 through February 2, 1977, made for a storm that anyone who lived through couldn't forget.

Irv made it into the station, but did so with panache.

"I couldn't get my car out, and I rode in on a horse. Some farmer, lent us a horse, and I rode onto the set riding a horse."

Buffalo State College Courier Express Collection/Staffannouncer Archives

Rick got an Amherst Police ride over to Tom Jolls' house, where the two hopped into the four-wheel drive truck of Tom's son Dale. It was a harrowing look at the Weather Outside that night, and when the siren of an ambulance pealed through Channel 7's Main and Utica neighborhood, many remember Tom's words.

"Pity the person who needs an ambulance on a night like tonight, but fortunate there is a driver who'd traverse the street to take the person to medical help."

Tom's home became a refuge of sorts for a neighbor family, whose home was positioned in such a way that it caught all the wind and the worst the blizzard had to offer.

"You couldn't really see outside, and you could hardly breathe the wind was so bad," remembers Tom.

IRV: BUFFALO'S ANCHORMAN!

It wasn't until the Blizzard of '85 that Mayor Griffin famously told Buffalonians to grab a six pack and stay inside, but it was an idea that Tom had during the big blizzard 8 years earlier. Son Dale, however, was not ready to oblige the Commander's request for a beer run at the height of the blizzard.

"Probably is the one storm that everyone remembers," says Irv. "There have been other bad storms, but nothing like that one. There wasn't that much snow that fell, actually, but there was a very stiff wind. The wind drove that snow into huge drifts. In some areas, the snow reached to the top of telephone poles."

Two-thousand cars were abandoned on Main Street downtown alone. President Carter declared Buffalo a *Federal Disaster Area*, and 23 people died as a result of the storm.

That storm, its aftermath, and death toll, really changed the way Buffalonians view weather and weather forecasts. It also changed the value placed on weather segments and weather anchors on television here.

"Before, you were just the TV weatherman," says Tom. "Now of course, you're a meteorologist. Once in a while these days, someone sneaks in who isn't a meteorologist, but the whole thing has changed dramatically since the Blizzard of '77."

"Weather up until that point was given the back seat. I was the end of the half hour news cast. If lucky, I was given 2 minutes at the end, because Irv pretty much ran the show, and news was important. "

"Rick and I would often ask for a little more time, especially when I'd end up with a minute and a half or something."

"Until the blizzard, weather was relegated to just being there, doing your forecast, very little embellishment. It was just strictly bang, bang, bang. "

"After the Blizzard, the weather became much more prominent. Now they lead the newscast when it gets cold out."

"Weather has become so important to people's lives, so if you don't inform them, you aren't doing your job. But there's that scare factor now."

"I was always afraid of overstepping a boundary. Little old ladies would tell me, those other weather guys, they scare me. I was always thinking, well, I don't want to scare anybody, but I don't want to leave anybody unprepared for what could happen. It was kind of a thin line there."

```
(HEAT)
    (BUFFALO, NEW YORK)---THE CITY OF BUFFALO GOT A REMINDER LAST NIGHT
THAT THIS SURGE OF MIDSUMMER HEAT HASN'T REALLY BEEN WITH US THAT LONG.
    TELEVISION STATION W-K-B-W SHOWED ITS LATE NEWS VIEWERS FILMS
OF A WINTER SNOWSTORM AND ASKED...'NOW WHAT WAS THAT YOU WERE SAYING
ABOUT THE HEAT?'
```

Irv's unusual style caught the fancy of an Associated Press reporter during an early 70s heat wave.

Weather Outside

There are other weather stories; other storms and heat waves, but most of Tom Jolls' stories have less to do with the weather, but more to do with "The Weather Outside" segment.

Channel 7 started broadcasting the weather segments from the sidewalk on Main Street right in front of the old studio before Tom got there in 1965.

"When I was still over at WBEN," remembers Tom, "they started doing the weather outside. We at Channel 4 thought it was a big joke, "Ahh, look at him standing outside, isn't that ridiculous?"

Tom picked up the franchise right from Main Street, until a car drove by with an occupant bearing what God gave him in an attempt at mooning *Eyewitness News* viewers.

With the studios still on Main Street, the Weather Outside then moved partially inside. Tom was still in the elements, but the cameras were inside, just on the other side of a garage door which went up for the weather segment.

IRV: BUFFALO'S ANCHORMAN!

It kept the cameras safe, but not necessarily the weather man.

"I remember one night in particular, I was doing a live Wonder Bread commercial in a raging snow storm. I mean, you could barely see me outside with the snow blowing."

"Irv usually had a kicker at the end of every newscast, but that night, he said, 'If you can think of anything funnier than a man doing a bread commercial in a raging blizzard, I can't think of anything!,' and that was it, that was the kicker that night."

Being out in the elements, and with a different sort of element nearby, was a completely different experience when Channel 7 moved the studios to Church Street in the late 70s.

The wind is much harsher there, nearly on the waterfront. For a while, the people were, too. Once prisoners inside the Erie County Holding Center realized they could scream and get on TV, they did.

Looking back, though, at almost 40 years of daily weather broadcasts outside, Tom is surprised at how few incidents there were, all told.

The ones that did happen, however, were certainly memorable. There were humping dogs and car alarms, thrown eggs and thrown snowballs, but the most memorable incidents involve humans *au natural*.

"I was mooned once, when we were on Main Street, but that never really made it on the air. One time a streaker came down, I could see him running at me out of the corner of my eye, and just as he was about to streak in front of the camera, the camera went back inside to the weather map showing temperatures. "

"So he never got on the air, but I can still remember him sitting at the guard's desk."

The man was sitting there, naked as a jaybird, curled in a ball, shivering. Ever the humanitarian, the Commander felt bad for the guy who tried to trounce his forecast with a weather stick of a different sort.

"He said, 'I bet a guy ten bucks that I could get on the air, and I didn't even get my ten bucks. "

Weather Stick
It was a quick conversation at a sporting goods store that really lead to one of the items Tom Jolls became best known for over the years.

"Of course, we got so much mileage out of the weather stick. That just 'happened.' Eastern Mountain Sports was the first in town to carry the weather stick. I had heard about it, and I went in to buy one."

"They saw me in there, and said, 'Oh I bet this thing tells the weather better than you guys do!'"

"I said ok, let's try it. In fact, the old Indians used it, and it's pretty simple science. When the moisture is heavy in the air before it rains, the thing is going to droop. When the air dries out, it's going to go up, and that's basically what it is."

Controversy erupted one day, as Tom went out to the weather gazebo to find the weather stick missing. It was apparently stolen. A big deal was made about it on the news and weather segments that day, more for fun than anything else.

Funnier still, was that an even bigger deal was made of replacing the purloined purveyor of precipitation.

"Msgr. Bill Gallagher felt so bad about our weather stick being stolen, that he came over, right down the street from the cathedral, with a new one for me. Well, the Bishop saw that, and he didn't think that it was a very good thing for the Monsignor to do, giving me this new weather stick."

It really wasn't all that surprising that it was stolen, as this slightly phallic dried out branch became the butt of dozens of Irv's jokes, and seemingly everybody had to have a weather stick. "They were selling them at Vidler's, and all over."

IRV: BUFFALO'S ANCHORMAN!

Salubrious
It was the one word you hope that Tom had in the forecast for the weekend. With that one word, you knew you were in for a great day.

"The word really has nothing to do with weather. It just means good, well being."

"When I used the word salubrious in the forecast, people knew it meant the weather was going to just be nice. The kind of day people like. Salubrious."

"It was a word that became associated with me. Viewers would send me postcards from Point Salubrious near the Thousand Islands."

Commander Tom
Sure, there was weather, but then there's the little matter of The Commander Tom Show. From 1965 to 1991, the children of Western New York and Southern Ontario tuned to Channel 7 for the man that was part super hero, part favorite uncle.

"Many times, I'll have people who watched Commander Tom as children come up to me and say, I didn't realize you did the weather until I was a teenager."

"It started back in 1965 when we first went on the air with the Superman Show," remembers Tom. "They needed a host, and thought, well, we'll put an Ike jacket on him, give him the title Commander."

Early on, Commander Tom had a few human sidekicks, none of which really seemed to fit. "I finally approached the manager one day, and said, 'Why don't I do something with puppets?' I had a lot of ideas for puppets, I had some voices that I could do, and there it began."

The best remembered is Dustmop, named after a pup from the Commander's childhood, but there was Cecily, the good witch; Sorcella, the bad witch; Ogle Stem Moose; Mattie the giraffe-alligator;

Tom Jolls Collection/Staffannouncer Archives

Jennifer Kurzdorfer/Tom Jolls Collection/Staffannouncer Archives

and of course, Furryburry creature, Commander Tom's nemesis—always around to annoy.

Each of these characters were given life by Commander Tom himself, who did the voices, came up with the personalities, and along with Mrs. Jolls, even handmade each of the puppets.

"My kids lost some toys," the Commander says, of the raw materials that made up some of Buffalo's most beloved television characters.

"One gave up a dog that became Dustmop; another gave up another animal that became another character. My wife and I fashioned these things, and came up with these puppets. I don't think my daughter ever forgave me for taking her dog away from her, but we had a lot of fun with that."

Controversy erupted in Western New York kiddom one day when Dustmop went missing from the CT show.

"A secretary at the station thought that the puppet was looking a little grungy, so she took it home to wash it. Well, Dustmop didn't make it."

On the air, the Commander told the kids that Dustmop had gone to a rejuvenation camp. It was the same story that was told about Promo the Robot, when a new costume was purchased for the co-star of Rocketship 7.

In the end, Dustmop kept his lovable personality and voice, but it was all in the form of a new, completely different puppet.

"We had three or four different Commander Tom uniforms. We started out with an Ike jacket, but when we went to color, that's when they got me the red Mountie jacket."

Channel 7, and especially Tom, paid special attention to the Canadian audience. It was a part-time job for "Miss Nan," also known as Mrs. Jolls, to handle the public appearances for the Commander, with a good many of those personal appearances coming north of the border. The Mountie jacket fit, then, for a couple of reasons.

Tom Jolls Collection/Staffannouncer Archives

"Part of it was because of the large Canadian audience, but part of it was that it was so colorful. I always did a lot of parades in Canada, and the OPP invariably would salute me, and I would feel so embarrassed."

Though his rank is forever *Commander* in the hearts and minds of generations of Buffalonians, the truth is, Tom is a humble enlisted man at heart.

"I was in the Army Signal Corps, and I never got better than a Specialist Third Class."

Buffalo State College Courier Express Collection/ Staff-announcer Archives

IRV: BUFFALO'S ANCHORMAN!

From a 1977 Eyewitness News Promo

Irv: Do you have this in blue?

Salesman 1: FanTAStic!

Salesman 2: Its.... its....

Salesman 1: Right! Would you mind repeating that again?

Irv: Do you have this in blue?

Salesman 2: No one's ever said it like that before!

Salesmen: (singing).... And that's why we say...

Irv Weinstein, you're really a pro...You got all the news, that we want to know...   You tell it like it is, and never throw us a curve, Nobody says it Like Irv.... Eyewitness News!

Chapter 7: Beyond the News

It's tough to imagine Buffalo of the 70s, 80s, and 90s without Irv Weinstein, just like it's tough to imagine Irv without Rick and Tom.

When Irv and his young family arrived in Buffalo in that old DeSoto back in 1958, he couldn't have known that 3 decades later he'd be a part of the fabric of the community.

"From the standpoint of where I was, Buffalo was the glowing city on the hill, a real toddlin' town. Things were really happening in Buffalo."

As a young man growing up in Rochester, Irv had some experience with Buffalo, enjoying the city's shows and restaurants. But after spending some time working in Buffalo, he found the area's greatest asset was something no economic downturn or political misman-agement could scuttle: The spirit of the people.

"One of the things that makes the Buffalo market a delight to work in, is that your audience is really tuned into what you're saying, or what you're showing. Because the city is buried under snow, or at the very least, extreme cold, for about 9 months of the year, they're not going outside to play tennis, or jog down the street. They're listening to radio. They're watching television."

"The day after a story ran, I'd have people say back to me, word for word, what was on the air the night before. So I knew that they were with us."

Though it's an overused expression, Irv, Rick, and Tom, over the decades they came into our homes, really did become like family.

"When I talk to people," says Irv, "when I receive correspondence from people, they talk about that *they had dinner with me*, every night; that I was a friend, and I'm glad."

"I think that is the highest compliment someone in broadcasting can ever get," says Irv, "that your audience thought that you were a part of the family. "

Buffalo State College Courier Express Collection/Staffannouncer Archives

It's a feeling that continues for each Irv, Rick, and Tom to this day.

"When I come back to Western New York after over a decade of retirement," says Irv, "one of the things I love is that it's a great ego booster. I walk into a grocery store or a restaurant, and it's like I never left. 'Hey Irv, how ya doin?' Some people think I never left. Some people tell me they watch me all the time, and I haven't been on in a decade."

It's something these working men had to come to grips with, a little bit anyway. Right after his retirement, Rick was having dinner at a diner in Amherst, and really didn't know how to take it when a waiter became almost inconsolable, gushing about the effect that he, Rick, had had on this waiter's life.

"It was hard for me to deal with; I had to ask him to stop. I was just a guy on TV. I had no idea that people would have these kinds of feelings about us," says Rick.

"That's when Irv and I started to talk about this kind of stuff, and try to understand this kind of thing. We think about that now, after the fact. I think it's one of the reasons we were so successful, because we didn't think about it then. It's who we are. It always has been. We're just who we are."

But unlike some Hollywood types or big name athletes, Irv would be disappointed if he knew you thought about saying 'hi' but didn't.

"I thrived on that, communicating with people," says Tom. "Looking back, I think about how lucky I was. Not just to do it all for a while, but to do it for close to 40 years; very, very fortunate.

"I've never shunned that part of the business, people saying hi, or wanting to chat. I knew it was going to part of the business, and I had to be gracious to these people, because that's what mattered: the people who were watching. If you weren't nice to them, then you aren't doing your whole job," says Tom, who loved meeting people at the Erie County Fair so much that they named the park from which he broadcast there "Tom Jolls Park."

Still to this day, Commander Tom loves when someone says hi or offers a kind word.

"It never fails to amaze me, and I always try to say to them, thank you for remembering. It's just so ingrained in people that they didn't forget. And that's just so nice."

You don't see him on TV with children anymore, but Commander Tom now spends more time with his own kids: Suzanne Bilson, T, Dale, Kathleen Burkholder, Lisa Murray, Timothy, Terry.

Buffalo State College Courier Express Collection/ Staff-announcer Archives

It gets a little complicated for the Commander occasionally.

"The funny thing for me is, nowadays, you never know if someone is going to remember you or not. Some people don't always say something right at the beginning. I went through a big project with a salesman a few weeks ago, I asked a lot of questions, and he was very helpful. Just before we parted and signed the deal, he made some off the cuff comment like, 'So how does it feel not to have to stand outside anymore?'"

"I wasn't sure that he had any inkling. After 10 years, a lot didn't watch, and a lot of people don't remember. People remembering makes it all worthwhile."

Irv says, "People ask, doesn't it bother you when people come up to you in a restaurant, or in line somewhere, and I say, 'Bother me?!? I love it!' Yes, the ratings are nice, but when people want to come over and talk to you, and feel that they can, it makes you feel like you must be doing something right. The satisfaction of having done a pretty good job; you can't buy that."

Part of the satisfaction for Irv was that it was such a varied group of people who would come up to him over the years.

"I knew that Buffalo was and is a very ethnic conscious community. Just look at the festivals and parades. Irish, Polish, Italian, Greek, and on and on. Generally, the people in those ethnic-type communities enjoy an individual who does something out of the box. And in a town where ethnicity is important, with a name like Irv Weinstein, I'm immediately identified as an ethnic person. And not necessarily Jewish, either. I was sort of like the universal guy, a universal anchor, everybody's anchor. Both from a philosophical stand point and a factual stand point. "

And that was true; the numbers bore out, for not just the blue collar guys down at the plant.

"The Eyewitness News audience was everybody. People would say to me, 'Yeah, Irv, you're alright, you have the guys at Bethlehem Steel,' but that's bull. Lawyers, doctors, psychiatrists."

People from all walks of life couldn't get enough of Irv, Rick, and Tom.

Buffalo State College Courier Express Collection/Staffannouncer Archives

"You talk about ratings, and at one point, we had higher ratings than the other two stations combined. That's phenomenal."

And again, that is not something that is lost on Irv.

"In the days before the remote control, people actually had to get up out of their chairs to change the station, and fine tune it, move the hanger on top of the set to get better reception. So viewers really had to want to see you at a specific time to get up and change the channel."

"It wasn't, 'Boy, look at us, guys...' We never felt like stars," says Rick. "We never realized until after we left, after the fact, the impact we were making in our community."

And it wasn't just Buffalo. An entire generation of Torontonians made their assumptions about Buffalo, Western New York, and even the United States as a whole based on *Eyewitness News*.

WIVB-TV reporter Rich Newberg discussed it with Irv during an interview.

"People sometimes equate Buffalo with Irv Weinstein," admitted Newberg who spent some time in direct competition with Irv when he anchored Channel 4's 6 o'clock newscasts.

"People in Toronto would sometime mock the newscasts, and the city," Newberg continued, "wondering if there was a Western New York town left that hadn't burned, or if there was a person walking around who hadn't been shot *at least* once..."

Irv responded with a laugh, "I would tell these Torontonians, *and I have,* don't be so snotty! It was just a roll of the dice that Buffalo had such a high number of wood frame constructions. Toronto had a huge fire years ago (The Great Toronto Fire of 1904) which burned much of the city's downtown. Buffalo actually sent fire fighting apparatus to help put out the blaze. To their credit, in Toronto, after that fire, an ordinance was passed limiting the amount of wood allowed in new structures in the city."

Buffalo State College Courier Express Collection/Staffannouncer Archives

But it's not all acrimony from Canada. Just as the stars of local Toronto and Hamilton televisions had and have a cult following in Western New York; Irv, too, is well loved on both sides of the border. Irv remembers a Toronto radio promotion ran on the basis of his popularity here and there.

"CHUM Radio ran a promotion in 1988, at a time when the US Presidential election and the Canadian Parliamentary election coincided. They decided to run a contest and run me for either President of the United States or Prime Minister of Canada. It was a lot of fun, spending a day on the media circuit in Toronto."

Irv fully admits that Toronto wasn't the only outside market that came calling for his services when *Eyewitness News* was one of the most highly rated newscasts in the country.

Buffalo State College Courier Express Collection/Staffannouncer Archives

"Over the years, I had some opportunities to leave for a lot more money. I learned something from my experiences in Waterloo, Iowa; and Parkersburg, West Virginia, and also the brief times I worked in Portland, Oregon and San Diego. What you learn is, when you have a good professional situation, that leaves you fulfilled and satisfied professionally, you can't buy that."

"There were anchor people making more money than me in the Buffalo market, even though I was number one in the ratings. Did it bother me? Yeah, but not enough to really make any difference."

It was a wonderful professional situation. But it was also that Buffalo provided a great place to raise a family. What was it like to call Irv Weinstein 'dad?'

Irv talked about his family, and his family about him, in an early 1980's broadcast of *PM Magazine*, at the time hosted in Buffalo by Debbie Stamp.

"If you compare me with Robert Young from *Father Knows Best* , I probably don't do too well," Irv said, "because early on in my career, when the children were small, I did not have a great deal of time to spend with them. And to be perfectly honest, on my days off, I wasn't the kind of dad who went out in the street and played ball. I have guilt feelings about the time I didn't spend with the children when they were small, and when I was trying to make it in this business."

As Debbie Stamp put it, "The Weinsteins lived not in a mansion, but in a typical house, in a typical neighborhood in Kenmore." Irv really is the typical guy we'd expect him to be watching him on television.

"I think my wife and I have an unusually good relationship. She has a very even disposition, as opposed to myself. I tend to be a little more volatile. Not as volatile as I used to be."

"She thinks I'm the funniest guy in the world. I broke her up from the moment we met, she just laughs and laughs, and when you're laughing, it's difficult to become angry."

"He's got a great sense of humor, and he's fun to live with," said Mrs. Weinstein of her husband. "I know his image is very often very businesslike and dignified, and he is that too, but, I was originally attracted to his sense of humor."

Cannoli on the Weather Outside Set
Irv Weinstein Collection/Staffannouncer Archives

IRV: BUFFALO'S ANCHORMAN!

The time since Irv, Rick and Tom sat together in our living rooms every night can now be measured in decades.

Rick Azar was the first to leave in 1989, making 25 years the mark to beat as the longest running anchor team in history. He'd been at Channel 7 since that first broadcast, 31 years before. Tom Jolls was the last to leave, a few months after Irv did in 1999.

On New Year's Eve 1998, Irv Weinstein ended his 34 year run at the helm of *Eyewitness News* with a heartfelt final sign off:

Finally... Yes, finally. Is there anyone in the western world who doesn't know that I'm retiring? Well apparently, there is. This e-mail arrived on our station manager's computer a couple of days ago. It reads, quote, 'I noticed on the TV tonight, on your channel logo saying Remembering Irv. I went to your internet page and there is no mention of your passing. Can you send me information on this?' End quote.

Well, sir, if you're watching, you'll notice that I appear to be alive, in a manner of speaking, anyway. Things have been a bit hectic, recently.

Now then, for the rest of you, I'd like to answer some questions that I've been getting since I announced that I'm retiring. Am I planning to move? No. Am I going to write a book? No. What am I going to do with myself? Well, I'm going to kick off my shoes and goof off. Read books, go to the movies weekday afternoons, watch lots of television news, spend lots of quality time with our children and grandchildren, and drive my wife crazy. The usual stuff.

Seriously though, friends, even though I'll no longer have a day job, I suspect that I'll pop up from time to time on television and radio, and I plan to continue to take an active role in the life of our community.

Now, it's time to thank some of the people without whom I would not have had the broadcast career that I had.

At the top of the list are my wife and children. Their unwavering love, support, encouragement, and honest criticism have always been there during the good times, and the not so good times.

And a big thank you to a couple of TV station managers, who hired me at the dawn of my career. If it wasn't for them, I might now be directing a cooking show in Waterloo, Iowa, or live wresting in Parkersburg, West Virginia.

I'm grateful to all the Buffalo and Canadian newspaper columnists, and radio and TV personalities, who, in the last few weeks, have showered me with the kind of accolades normally reserved for people who break sports records or walk on the moon.

None of the last four decades would have happened for me without the owners, managers, and staff at WKBW Radio and Television, who were, and are, the best in the business.

But you, you the viewers were the key element whatever success I've achieved. We connected, on and off the air, you and me. I can never thank you enough. You made all of my dreams come true. May all of yours come true as well. Good night.

I once asked Irv about his legacy.

"You don't think about everything you do, every single day. It's a compilation of weeks, and months, and years of work that you hope has had some impact on people. And when it appears that it does, and that it has, it's a very rewarding thing."

"I was the original Irv Weinstein, that's all I was really. Each person represents a particular talent, a particular ability. The impact I had in the market, may have set a fairly high watermark in the marketplace.

"For that, I am very grateful."

Tom's final words on the weather outside: "May all your days be salubrious." A wonderful thought and one he meant from the bottom of his heart.

In many respects, it was a unique relationship Irv, Rick, and Tom shared, one not too different from brotherhood. One that continues to this day.

"We now keep in contact constantly over e-mail," says Tom. "We were all together last summer, at Chef's. It was the first time were together, all of us, in 14 years. We've seen each other separately of course, 14 years since we'd all been together. It was great, and it was like we'd never been apart. It was the same relationship there, and it will never go away."

"We laugh, we cry. I can still make him cry at the drop of a hat," Rick says of Irv. "Like a bag of mush. He comes on like this tough news guy, but he's a mush. We're in touch every day."

Irv, Rick, and Tom. They really love each other. And we love them.

Groundbreaking for 'the House That Irv Built.' Congressman John LaFalce, County Executive Ned Regan, Mayor Stanley Makowski, and WKBW GM Phil Beuth at the future home of Channel 7. 1977. Buffalo State College Courier Express Collection/ Staffannouncer Archives

About the author

Steve Cichon is an award-winning journalist, author, and historian. *The Buffalo News* calls him "A true Buffalonian," and says "he knows this town."

The winner of a *Buffalo Business First '40 Under 40'* Award in 2010 and dozens of Associated Press Awards as an anchor and reporter with WBEN Radio since 2003, Steve has worked in radio and television in Buffalo since 1993.

Cichon's 2009 book, 'The Complete History of Parkside,' was described by *Western New York Heritage Magazine* as 'packed with numerous facts from start to finish, (A) fun read through one of the city's most beautiful residential neighborhoods.' Steve and his wife Monica (above) are the care-takers of their 1909 EB Green home in Buffalo's Parkside Neighborhood.

While Steve has spent years collecting the Irv, Rick, and Tom story, his interests also extend to the history of all of Buffalo and Western New York as well. He's the curator, writer, and webmaster at *staffannouncer.com*, a website dedicated to preserving and sharing the Buffalo area's pop culture history, particularly the history of Buffalo radio and television, and the numerous untold stories of everyday living on the Niagara Frontier.

Steve has served on numerous non-profit boards, and volunteers his

time liberally with a handful of civic, charitable, and church groups, and likes working on projects which don't involve meetings. (He'd rather 'do' than meet!)
Steve with Irv, Rick, &Tom, 1998

Acknowledgements....

I've spoken, corresponded with, and interviewed Irv Weinstein, Rick Azar, and Tom Jolls dozens of times, and listened to their stories.

I've also spent most of my life collecting stories and interviews Irv, Rick and Tom have given to others. Some of those are explained on this page, some authors and interviewers are thanked on the coming pages, as are many who've given me materials over the years.

Irv, Rick, and Tom spoke at length to WNED-TV for a 2010 documentary "Don't Touch That Dial." Irv also spoke with Channel 17 for a 1977 documentary "The Struggle to Win at 6 & 11."

The induction speech of Irv, Rick and Tom into the Buffalo Broadcast Pioneers Hall of Fame in 1997; An Irv interview with Debbie Stamp on PM Magazine in the early 80's; An Irv appearance on the *Majic 102 Morning Show* with Sandy Beach in 1988.

Rick Azar has appeared on several shows I produced over the years, and I referred back to those tapes. He was on the WNSA Sports Symposium, and also on WNSA with Mike Schopp in 2001. Rick appeared with Chris Parker on WBEN's One-On-One Sports in 1997.

Tom's 1996 book "Western New York Weather Guide" included some great stories upon which I was able to ask Tom to elaborate.

I referred to several interviews that were given at the time of Irv's retirement; most notably an hour-long in-studio appearance on Tom Bauerle's *Breakfast with Bauerle* show on WGR Radio.

Irv's last newscast on WKBW-TV on December 31, 1998, was also invaluable; particularly the story produced by Eyewitness News Reporter Steve Boyd and videographer Scott McDowell about stories Irv has covered.

I also referred to several interviews Irv, Rick and Tom have granted me through the years, either for stories for WBEN Radio, WNSA Radio, staffannouncer.com, or the Buffalo Broadcast Pioneers, as well as more casual conversations or e-mail exchanges with each through the years. These interactions acted as the foundation for the story presented here.

Irv sat down with Rich Newberg, Don Yearke & me for 2 hours at his Ellicottville home in May, 2009. Referring to this conversation helped bridge many gaps and fill in many holes.

I also spent several hours with Tom Jolls at his Orchard Park home in January 2011, and spoke at length over the phone with Rick Azar from his North Carolina home during the spring of 2011.

The Courier-Express Archives are housed at The Buffalo State College Archives and Special Collections. Dan DiLandro went way beyond the call of duty to find photos for use in this book. His level of enthusiasm for this project was key in the final product you hold in your hands.

ForgottenBuffalo.com is also a tremendous resource on Buffalo's pop culture history. The bountiful resources and archives of Forgotten Buffalo are never more than a phone call or e-mail away, and I rely on them heavily.

Randy Bushover and my wife Monica edited this book, and found at least 149 corrections that had to be made right before it went to print. Irv, Rick, and Tom also pointed out some corrections, additions, and subtractions that had to be made in the (almost!) final draft.

Thanks... Dan DiLandro, Don Yearke, Rich Newberg, Al Wallack, the late Al Ancombe, Jennifer Kurzdorfer, Lynne Bader-Gregory, Larry Felser, John Di Scuillo, the late Jim Kelley, Alan Pergament, Gary Deeb, Jim Baker, Paul Kovacs, Howard Goldman, Mike Randall, John Bisci, Tom Langmyer, Rev. John P. Mack, Msgr. Francis Braun, Kevin Keenan, Dave Gillen, Matt Sanfilippo, Sandy Beach, Tom Bauerle, Steve Boyd, Scott McDowell, Chris Parker, Mike Schopp, John Zach, Mary Kunz Goldman, John Demerle, Bob Koshinski, the late Ed Little, and Elaine Weinstein, Edith Carballada, and Janice Jolls... aka Mrs. Irv, Rick, and Tom.

To my late dad, who *'couldn't stand John Beard'* (sorry John!) when he was on Channel 4, which meant plenty sitting on dad's lap watching Irv as a little kid in the late 70s and early 80s; My mom, who reminds anyone who'll listen that even before I could speak in complete words, I excitedly wanted to watch *Irv Tine-Tine,* and to my whole family: The Cichons, the Coyles, the Huxleys, the Martynas, the Bujedas, and all the rest. You guys are the best.

To Van Miller, for the added impetus,

To Max the Dog (RIP) and Willow the Dog, each of whom added weeks to this project with their loving nudges and desperate pleas for attention and petting,

To three people without whom I couldn't have written this book:

My wife **Monica**, my best friend, who only barely complained about being nearly abandoned a few times while I poured energy and time into this project, and then did a most thorough edit job;

Brian Meyer, who distributes this book, and is a trusted friend and resource, and helps dozens of local authors write books without losing scads of money;

and **Marty Biniasz**, my partner in crime and fellow Buffalo Pop Culture Historian, the only man I know to share the same passion I have in the love of all things that make Buffalo, Buffalo.

And the biggest thanks of all… to the greatest anchor team in history:

Irv, Rick, & Tom.

STEVE CICHON

Order copies of this and other books online
at staffannouncer.com!

Other Buffalo books from Steve Cichon & staffannouncer.com:

The Complete History of Parkside, Buffalo, NY...... $14.95

The Real Steve Cichon: A Tribute to My Ol'Man...... $12.95

Initially created as a website to share Steve's thousands of images and sounds from Buffalo's radio and TV past, staffannouncer.com has grown to become an online celebration of Buffalo's pop-culture history, devoted to bringing to the World Wide Web the people, places and thoughts of Buffalo that you won't find anywhere else on the internet, and it's all done with Steve's sense of history and sense of humor.

Over half a million visitors have enjoyed Steve's virtual strolls down Buffalo's memory lane since 2003.